TIME MASTERY AND BLOCKER

Goals Realized with Intention and Certainty

Clarity. Commitment. Completion.

ISBN 978-1-971308-02-09

Welcome to the Time Mastery and Blocker

A sanctuary where your dreams meet strategy, and your essence finds expression in the tangible beauty of your life's purpose.

Time Mastery and Blocker is not a productivity book. It is a guide to conscious creation—where time becomes an ally, not a source of pressure, and goals are realized with intention, certainty, and inner alignment.

At its core, this book is about mastery from the inside out. True time mastery begins with clarity—knowing what matters, why it matters, and who you are choosing to be as you pursue it. From that place, commitment becomes natural, not forced, and action becomes focused, At the heart of the Time Mastery and Blocker is a simple yet powerful truth: the most reliable way to predict your future is to create it—intentionally. When clarity leads, commitment deepens, and completion becomes inevitable.

You are a precious and irreplaceable expression of life. This book honors that truth by helping you move beyond busyness and into purposeful action. Through intentional time blocking, reflective visioning, and structured planning, you will learn how to work with time rather than against it—transforming it into a trusted ally in the realization of your goals.

Within these pages, you'll discover essential elements for:

Visioning and Goal Setting — grounding your aspirations in meaning, alignment, and purpose

Time Mastery — applying the transformative time-blocking method taught in the Time Mastery programs

Time Blocking — dissolving the internal and external patterns that disrupt focus, energy, and follow-through by blocking time for what matters most.

Accompanied by resources such as the Power Movers Planner, Meeting Notebook, and Genius Moments Journal, this work serves as your compass—guiding you toward focused execution and meaningful impact.

Each day begins with a knowing: a singular gift lives within you. With that awareness, you are empowered to plan boldly, act decisively, and complete what matters most.

Cheers to your brilliance, your boldness, and the extraordinary life you are creating!

TIME MASTERY AND BLOCKER

Goals Realized with Intention and Certainty

Clarity. Commitment. Completion.

Goal Planner Time Mastery
by ThinkVirtues®
Find more Planners, Workbooks, and
a Master Collection of Virtues at ThinkVirtues.com

TIME MASTERY AND BLOCKER

Goal #1	Result
Why I wanted it	Reward if achieved

Goal #2	Result
Why I wanted it	Reward if achieved

Goal #3	Result
Why I wanted it	Reward if achieved

Goal #4	Result
Why I wanted it	Reward if achieved

Goal #5	Result
Why I wanted it	Reward if achieved

Thoughts become words. Words become action. Actions become character. Character becomes destiny.

Goal #6	Result
Why I wanted it	Reward if achieved

Goal #7	Result
Why I wanted it	Reward if achieved

Goal #8	Result
Why I wanted it	Reward if achieved

Goal #9	Result
Why I wanted it	Reward if achieved

Goal #10	Result
Why I wanted it	Reward if achieved

Goal #11	Result
Why I wanted it	Reward if achieved

Goal #12	Result
Why I wanted it	Reward if achieved

Goal #13	Result
Why I wanted it	Reward if achieved

Goal #14	Result
Why I wanted it	Reward if achieved

Goal #15	Result
Why I wanted it	Reward if achieved

Goal #16	Result
Why I wanted it	Reward if achieved

Goal #17	Result
Why I wanted it	Reward if achieved

Goal #18	Result
Why I wanted it	Reward if achieved

Goal #19	Result
Why I wanted it	Reward if achieved

Goal #20	Result
Why I wanted it	Reward if achieved

NOTES

Note #1	
Main point	Outcome

Note #2	
Main point	Outcome

Note #3	
Main point	Outcome

Note #4	
Main point	Outcome

Note #5	
Main point	Outcome

Action Step #1

Action Step #2

Action Step #3

Action Step #4

Action Step #5

NOTES

Thoughts become words. Words become action. Actions become character. Character becomes destiny.

DAY / DATE ______________________________

MY GOALS TODAY

____

____

____

____

____

____

NOTES

TIME BLOCKS

3:00 am	3:30 am
4:00 am	4:30 am
5:00 am	5:30 am
6:00 am	6:30 am
7:00 am	7:30 am
8:00 am	8:30 am
9:00 am	9:30 am
10:00 am	10:30 am
11:00 am	11:30 am
12:00 pm	12:30 pm
1:00 pm	1:30 pm
2:00 pm	2:30 pm
3:00 pm	3:30 pm
4:00 pm	4:30 pm
5:00 pm	5:30 pm
6:00 pm	6:30 pm
7:00 pm	7:30 pm
8:00 pm	8:30 pm
9:00 pm	9:30 pm

Thoughts become words. Words become action. Actions become character. Character becomes destiny.

TIME MASTERY AND BLOCKER

DAY / DATE ______________________

MY GOALS TODAY

____

____

____

____

____

____

NOTES

TIME BLOCKS

3:00 am	3:30 am
4:00 am	4:30 am
5:00 am	5:30 am
6:00 am	6:30 am
7:00 am	7:30 am
8:00 am	8:30 am
9:00 am	9:30 am
10:00 am	10:30 am
11:00 am	11:30 am
12:00 pm	12:30 pm
1:00 pm	1:30 pm
2:00 pm	2:30 pm
3:00 pm	3:30 pm
4:00 pm	4:30 pm
5:00 pm	5:30 pm
6:00 pm	6:30 pm
7:00 pm	7:30 pm
8:00 pm	8:30 pm
9:00 pm	9:30 pm

DAY / DATE ______________________________

MY GOALS TODAY

____

____

____

____

____

____

NOTES

TIME BLOCKS

3:00 am	3:30 am
4:00 am	4:30 am
5:00 am	5:30 am
6:00 am	6:30 am
7:00 am	7:30 am
8:00 am	8:30 am
9:00 am	9:30 am
10:00 am	10:30 am
11:00 am	11:30 am
12:00 pm	12:30 pm
1:00 pm	1:30 pm
2:00 pm	2:30 pm
3:00 pm	3:30 pm
4:00 pm	4:30 pm
5:00 pm	5:30 pm
6:00 pm	6:30 pm
7:00 pm	7:30 pm
8:00 pm	8:30 pm
9:00 pm	9:30 pm

DAY / DATE ______________________________

MY GOALS TODAY

____

____

____

____

____

____

NOTES

TIME BLOCKS

3:00 am	3:30 am
4:00 am	4:30 am
5:00 am	5:30 am
6:00 am	6:30 am
7:00 am	7:30 am
8:00 am	8:30 am
9:00 am	9:30 am
10:00 am	10:30 am
11:00 am	11:30 am
12:00 pm	12:30 pm
1:00 pm	1:30 pm
2:00 pm	2:30 pm
3:00 pm	3:30 pm
4:00 pm	4:30 pm
5:00 pm	5:30 pm
6:00 pm	6:30 pm
7:00 pm	7:30 pm
8:00 pm	8:30 pm
9:00 pm	9:30 pm

DAY / DATE ______________________________

MY GOALS TODAY

____

____

____

____

____

____

NOTES

TIME BLOCKS

3:00 am	3:30 am
4:00 am	4:30 am
5:00 am	5:30 am
6:00 am	6:30 am
7:00 am	7:30 am
8:00 am	8:30 am
9:00 am	9:30 am
10:00 am	10:30 am
11:00 am	11:30 am
12:00 pm	12:30 pm
1:00 pm	1:30 pm
2:00 pm	2:30 pm
3:00 pm	3:30 pm
4:00 pm	4:30 pm
5:00 pm	5:30 pm
6:00 pm	6:30 pm
7:00 pm	7:30 pm
8:00 pm	8:30 pm
9:00 pm	9:30 pm

DAY / DATE ______________________________

MY GOALS TODAY

____

____

____

____

____

____

NOTES

TIME BLOCKS

3:00 am	3:30 am
4:00 am	4:30 am
5:00 am	5:30 am
6:00 am	6:30 am
7:00 am	7:30 am
8:00 am	8:30 am
9:00 am	9:30 am
10:00 am	10:30 am
11:00 am	11:30 am
12:00 pm	12:30 pm
1:00 pm	1:30 pm
2:00 pm	2:30 pm
3:00 pm	3:30 pm
4:00 pm	4:30 pm
5:00 pm	5:30 pm
6:00 pm	6:30 pm
7:00 pm	7:30 pm
8:00 pm	8:30 pm
9:00 pm	9:30 pm

DAY / DATE ______________________________

MY GOALS TODAY

____
____
____
____
____
____

NOTES

TIME BLOCKS

3:00 am	3:30 am
4:00 am	4:30 am
5:00 am	5:30 am
6:00 am	6:30 am
7:00 am	7:30 am
8:00 am	8:30 am
9:00 am	9:30 am
10:00 am	10:30 am
11:00 am	11:30 am
12:00 pm	12:30 pm
1:00 pm	1:30 pm
2:00 pm	2:30 pm
3:00 pm	3:30 pm
4:00 pm	4:30 pm
5:00 pm	5:30 pm
6:00 pm	6:30 pm
7:00 pm	7:30 pm
8:00 pm	8:30 pm
9:00 pm	9:30 pm

DAY / DATE ______________________________

MY GOALS TODAY

____
____
____
____
____
____

NOTES

TIME BLOCKS

3:00 am	3:30 am
4:00 am	4:30 am
5:00 am	5:30 am
6:00 am	6:30 am
7:00 am	7:30 am
8:00 am	8:30 am
9:00 am	9:30 am
10:00 am	10:30 am
11:00 am	11:30 am
12:00 pm	12:30 pm
1:00 pm	1:30 pm
2:00 pm	2:30 pm
3:00 pm	3:30 pm
4:00 pm	4:30 pm
5:00 pm	5:30 pm
6:00 pm	6:30 pm
7:00 pm	7:30 pm
8:00 pm	8:30 pm
9:00 pm	9:30 pm

DAY / DATE ______________________________

MY GOALS TODAY

____
____
____
____
____
____

NOTES

TIME BLOCKS

3:00 am	3:30 am
4:00 am	4:30 am
5:00 am	5:30 am
6:00 am	6:30 am
7:00 am	7:30 am
8:00 am	8:30 am
9:00 am	9:30 am
10:00 am	10:30 am
11:00 am	11:30 am
12:00 pm	12:30 pm
1:00 pm	1:30 pm
2:00 pm	2:30 pm
3:00 pm	3:30 pm
4:00 pm	4:30 pm
5:00 pm	5:30 pm
6:00 pm	6:30 pm
7:00 pm	7:30 pm
8:00 pm	8:30 pm
9:00 pm	9:30 pm

DAY / DATE ____________________

MY GOALS TODAY

____

____

____

____

____

____

NOTES

TIME BLOCKS

3:00 am	3:30 am
4:00 am	4:30 am
5:00 am	5:30 am
6:00 am	6:30 am
7:00 am	7:30 am
8:00 am	8:30 am
9:00 am	9:30 am
10:00 am	10:30 am
11:00 am	11:30 am
12:00 pm	12:30 pm
1:00 pm	1:30 pm
2:00 pm	2:30 pm
3:00 pm	3:30 pm
4:00 pm	4:30 pm
5:00 pm	5:30 pm
6:00 pm	6:30 pm
7:00 pm	7:30 pm
8:00 pm	8:30 pm
9:00 pm	9:30 pm

DAY / DATE ____________________

MY GOALS TODAY

____

____

____

____

____

____

NOTES

TIME BLOCKS

3:00 am	3:30 am
4:00 am	4:30 am
5:00 am	5:30 am
6:00 am	6:30 am
7:00 am	7:30 am
8:00 am	8:30 am
9:00 am	9:30 am
10:00 am	10:30 am
11:00 am	11:30 am
12:00 pm	12:30 pm
1:00 pm	1:30 pm
2:00 pm	2:30 pm
3:00 pm	3:30 pm
4:00 pm	4:30 pm
5:00 pm	5:30 pm
6:00 pm	6:30 pm
7:00 pm	7:30 pm
8:00 pm	8:30 pm
9:00 pm	9:30 pm

DAY / DATE ____

MY GOALS TODAY

____

____

____

____

____

____

NOTES

TIME BLOCKS

3:00 am	3:30 am
4:00 am	4:30 am
5:00 am	5:30 am
6:00 am	6:30 am
7:00 am	7:30 am
8:00 am	8:30 am
9:00 am	9:30 am
10:00 am	10:30 am
11:00 am	11:30 am
12:00 pm	12:30 pm
1:00 pm	1:30 pm
2:00 pm	2:30 pm
3:00 pm	3:30 pm
4:00 pm	4:30 pm
5:00 pm	5:30 pm
6:00 pm	6:30 pm
7:00 pm	7:30 pm
8:00 pm	8:30 pm
9:00 pm	9:30 pm

DAY / DATE ____________________

MY GOALS TODAY

____
____
____
____
____
____

NOTES

TIME BLOCKS

3:00 am	3:30 am
4:00 am	4:30 am
5:00 am	5:30 am
6:00 am	6:30 am
7:00 am	7:30 am
8:00 am	8:30 am
9:00 am	9:30 am
10:00 am	10:30 am
11:00 am	11:30 am
12:00 pm	12:30 pm
1:00 pm	1:30 pm
2:00 pm	2:30 pm
3:00 pm	3:30 pm
4:00 pm	4:30 pm
5:00 pm	5:30 pm
6:00 pm	6:30 pm
7:00 pm	7:30 pm
8:00 pm	8:30 pm
9:00 pm	9:30 pm

DAY / DATE ____________________

MY GOALS TODAY

____

____

____

____

____

____

NOTES

TIME BLOCKS

3:00 am	3:30 am
4:00 am	4:30 am
5:00 am	5:30 am
6:00 am	6:30 am
7:00 am	7:30 am
8:00 am	8:30 am
9:00 am	9:30 am
10:00 am	10:30 am
11:00 am	11:30 am
12:00 pm	12:30 pm
1:00 pm	1:30 pm
2:00 pm	2:30 pm
3:00 pm	3:30 pm
4:00 pm	4:30 pm
5:00 pm	5:30 pm
6:00 pm	6:30 pm
7:00 pm	7:30 pm
8:00 pm	8:30 pm
9:00 pm	9:30 pm

DAY / DATE ______________________

MY GOALS TODAY

____
____
____
____
____
____

NOTES

TIME BLOCKS

3:00 am	3:30 am
4:00 am	4:30 am
5:00 am	5:30 am
6:00 am	6:30 am
7:00 am	7:30 am
8:00 am	8:30 am
9:00 am	9:30 am
10:00 am	10:30 am
11:00 am	11:30 am
12:00 pm	12:30 pm
1:00 pm	1:30 pm
2:00 pm	2:30 pm
3:00 pm	3:30 pm
4:00 pm	4:30 pm
5:00 pm	5:30 pm
6:00 pm	6:30 pm
7:00 pm	7:30 pm
8:00 pm	8:30 pm
9:00 pm	9:30 pm

DAY / DATE ____________________

MY GOALS TODAY

____

____

____

____

____

____

NOTES

TIME BLOCKS

3:00 am	3:30 am
4:00 am	4:30 am
5:00 am	5:30 am
6:00 am	6:30 am
7:00 am	7:30 am
8:00 am	8:30 am
9:00 am	9:30 am
10:00 am	10:30 am
11:00 am	11:30 am
12:00 pm	12:30 pm
1:00 pm	1:30 pm
2:00 pm	2:30 pm
3:00 pm	3:30 pm
4:00 pm	4:30 pm
5:00 pm	5:30 pm
6:00 pm	6:30 pm
7:00 pm	7:30 pm
8:00 pm	8:30 pm
9:00 pm	9:30 pm

Thoughts become words. Words become action. Actions become character. Character becomes destiny.

DAY / DATE ______________________________

MY GOALS TODAY

____

____

____

____

____

____

NOTES

TIME BLOCKS

3:00 am	3:30 am
4:00 am	4:30 am
5:00 am	5:30 am
6:00 am	6:30 am
7:00 am	7:30 am
8:00 am	8:30 am
9:00 am	9:30 am
10:00 am	10:30 am
11:00 am	11:30 am
12:00 pm	12:30 pm
1:00 pm	1:30 pm
2:00 pm	2:30 pm
3:00 pm	3:30 pm
4:00 pm	4:30 pm
5:00 pm	5:30 pm
6:00 pm	6:30 pm
7:00 pm	7:30 pm
8:00 pm	8:30 pm
9:00 pm	9:30 pm

DAY / DATE ____________________

MY GOALS TODAY

____
____
____
____
____
____

NOTES

TIME BLOCKS

3:00 am	3:30 am
4:00 am	4:30 am
5:00 am	5:30 am
6:00 am	6:30 am
7:00 am	7:30 am
8:00 am	8:30 am
9:00 am	9:30 am
10:00 am	10:30 am
11:00 am	11:30 am
12:00 pm	12:30 pm
1:00 pm	1:30 pm
2:00 pm	2:30 pm
3:00 pm	3:30 pm
4:00 pm	4:30 pm
5:00 pm	5:30 pm
6:00 pm	6:30 pm
7:00 pm	7:30 pm
8:00 pm	8:30 pm
9:00 pm	9:30 pm

DAY / DATE ______________________________

MY GOALS TODAY

____

____

____

____

____

____

NOTES

TIME BLOCKS

3:00 am	3:30 am
4:00 am	4:30 am
5:00 am	5:30 am
6:00 am	6:30 am
7:00 am	7:30 am
8:00 am	8:30 am
9:00 am	9:30 am
10:00 am	10:30 am
11:00 am	11:30 am
12:00 pm	12:30 pm
1:00 pm	1:30 pm
2:00 pm	2:30 pm
3:00 pm	3:30 pm
4:00 pm	4:30 pm
5:00 pm	5:30 pm
6:00 pm	6:30 pm
7:00 pm	7:30 pm
8:00 pm	8:30 pm
9:00 pm	9:30 pm

TIME MASTERY AND BLOCKER

DAY / DATE ____________________

MY GOALS TODAY

____

____

____

____

____

____

NOTES

TIME BLOCKS

3:00 am	3:30 am
4:00 am	4:30 am
5:00 am	5:30 am
6:00 am	6:30 am
7:00 am	7:30 am
8:00 am	8:30 am
9:00 am	9:30 am
10:00 am	10:30 am
11:00 am	11:30 am
12:00 pm	12:30 pm
1:00 pm	1:30 pm
2:00 pm	2:30 pm
3:00 pm	3:30 pm
4:00 pm	4:30 pm
5:00 pm	5:30 pm
6:00 pm	6:30 pm
7:00 pm	7:30 pm
8:00 pm	8:30 pm
9:00 pm	9:30 pm

Thoughts become words. Words become action. Actions become character. Character becomes destiny.

DAY / DATE ____________________

MY GOALS TODAY

____

____

____

____

____

____

NOTES

TIME BLOCKS

3:00 am	3:30 am
4:00 am	4:30 am
5:00 am	5:30 am
6:00 am	6:30 am
7:00 am	7:30 am
8:00 am	8:30 am
9:00 am	9:30 am
10:00 am	10:30 am
11:00 am	11:30 am
12:00 pm	12:30 pm
1:00 pm	1:30 pm
2:00 pm	2:30 pm
3:00 pm	3:30 pm
4:00 pm	4:30 pm
5:00 pm	5:30 pm
6:00 pm	6:30 pm
7:00 pm	7:30 pm
8:00 pm	8:30 pm
9:00 pm	9:30 pm

DAY / DATE ______________________________

MY GOALS TODAY

____

____

____

____

____

____

NOTES

TIME BLOCKS

3:00 am	3:30 am
4:00 am	4:30 am
5:00 am	5:30 am
6:00 am	6:30 am
7:00 am	7:30 am
8:00 am	8:30 am
9:00 am	9:30 am
10:00 am	10:30 am
11:00 am	11:30 am
12:00 pm	12:30 pm
1:00 pm	1:30 pm
2:00 pm	2:30 pm
3:00 pm	3:30 pm
4:00 pm	4:30 pm
5:00 pm	5:30 pm
6:00 pm	6:30 pm
7:00 pm	7:30 pm
8:00 pm	8:30 pm
9:00 pm	9:30 pm

DAY / DATE ________________________________

MY GOALS TODAY

____
____
____
____
____
____

NOTES

TIME BLOCKS

3:00 am	3:30 am
4:00 am	4:30 am
5:00 am	5:30 am
6:00 am	6:30 am
7:00 am	7:30 am
8:00 am	8:30 am
9:00 am	9:30 am
10:00 am	10:30 am
11:00 am	11:30 am
12:00 pm	12:30 pm
1:00 pm	1:30 pm
2:00 pm	2:30 pm
3:00 pm	3:30 pm
4:00 pm	4:30 pm
5:00 pm	5:30 pm
6:00 pm	6:30 pm
7:00 pm	7:30 pm
8:00 pm	8:30 pm
9:00 pm	9:30 pm

DAY / DATE ______________________________

MY GOALS TODAY

____

____

____

____

____

____

NOTES

TIME BLOCKS

3:00 am	3:30 am
4:00 am	4:30 am
5:00 am	5:30 am
6:00 am	6:30 am
7:00 am	7:30 am
8:00 am	8:30 am
9:00 am	9:30 am
10:00 am	10:30 am
11:00 am	11:30 am
12:00 pm	12:30 pm
1:00 pm	1:30 pm
2:00 pm	2:30 pm
3:00 pm	3:30 pm
4:00 pm	4:30 pm
5:00 pm	5:30 pm
6:00 pm	6:30 pm
7:00 pm	7:30 pm
8:00 pm	8:30 pm
9:00 pm	9:30 pm

DAY / DATE ____________________

MY GOALS TODAY

____
____
____
____
____
____

NOTES

TIME BLOCKS

3:00 am	3:30 am
4:00 am	4:30 am
5:00 am	5:30 am
6:00 am	6:30 am
7:00 am	7:30 am
8:00 am	8:30 am
9:00 am	9:30 am
10:00 am	10:30 am
11:00 am	11:30 am
12:00 pm	12:30 pm
1:00 pm	1:30 pm
2:00 pm	2:30 pm
3:00 pm	3:30 pm
4:00 pm	4:30 pm
5:00 pm	5:30 pm
6:00 pm	6:30 pm
7:00 pm	7:30 pm
8:00 pm	8:30 pm
9:00 pm	9:30 pm

DAY / DATE ______________________________

MY GOALS TODAY

____
____
____
____
____
____

NOTES

TIME BLOCKS

3:00 am	3:30 am
4:00 am	4:30 am
5:00 am	5:30 am
6:00 am	6:30 am
7:00 am	7:30 am
8:00 am	8:30 am
9:00 am	9:30 am
10:00 am	10:30 am
11:00 am	11:30 am
12:00 pm	12:30 pm
1:00 pm	1:30 pm
2:00 pm	2:30 pm
3:00 pm	3:30 pm
4:00 pm	4:30 pm
5:00 pm	5:30 pm
6:00 pm	6:30 pm
7:00 pm	7:30 pm
8:00 pm	8:30 pm
9:00 pm	9:30 pm

DAY / DATE ______________________________

MY GOALS TODAY

____

____

____

____

____

____

NOTES

TIME BLOCKS

3:00 am	3:30 am
4:00 am	4:30 am
5:00 am	5:30 am
6:00 am	6:30 am
7:00 am	7:30 am
8:00 am	8:30 am
9:00 am	9:30 am
10:00 am	10:30 am
11:00 am	11:30 am
12:00 pm	12:30 pm
1:00 pm	1:30 pm
2:00 pm	2:30 pm
3:00 pm	3:30 pm
4:00 pm	4:30 pm
5:00 pm	5:30 pm
6:00 pm	6:30 pm
7:00 pm	7:30 pm
8:00 pm	8:30 pm
9:00 pm	9:30 pm

DAY / DATE ______________________________

MY GOALS TODAY

____
____
____
____
____
____

NOTES

TIME BLOCKS

3:00 am	3:30 am
4:00 am	4:30 am
5:00 am	5:30 am
6:00 am	6:30 am
7:00 am	7:30 am
8:00 am	8:30 am
9:00 am	9:30 am
10:00 am	10:30 am
11:00 am	11:30 am
12:00 pm	12:30 pm
1:00 pm	1:30 pm
2:00 pm	2:30 pm
3:00 pm	3:30 pm
4:00 pm	4:30 pm
5:00 pm	5:30 pm
6:00 pm	6:30 pm
7:00 pm	7:30 pm
8:00 pm	8:30 pm
9:00 pm	9:30 pm

DAY / DATE ____________________

MY GOALS TODAY

____
____
____
____
____
____

NOTES

TIME BLOCKS

3:00 am	3:30 am
4:00 am	4:30 am
5:00 am	5:30 am
6:00 am	6:30 am
7:00 am	7:30 am
8:00 am	8:30 am
9:00 am	9:30 am
10:00 am	10:30 am
11:00 am	11:30 am
12:00 pm	12:30 pm
1:00 pm	1:30 pm
2:00 pm	2:30 pm
3:00 pm	3:30 pm
4:00 pm	4:30 pm
5:00 pm	5:30 pm
6:00 pm	6:30 pm
7:00 pm	7:30 pm
8:00 pm	8:30 pm
9:00 pm	9:30 pm

DAY / DATE ______________________________

MY GOALS TODAY

____

____

____

____

____

____

NOTES

TIME BLOCKS

3:00 am	3:30 am
4:00 am	4:30 am
5:00 am	5:30 am
6:00 am	6:30 am
7:00 am	7:30 am
8:00 am	8:30 am
9:00 am	9:30 am
10:00 am	10:30 am
11:00 am	11:30 am
12:00 pm	12:30 pm
1:00 pm	1:30 pm
2:00 pm	2:30 pm
3:00 pm	3:30 pm
4:00 pm	4:30 pm
5:00 pm	5:30 pm
6:00 pm	6:30 pm
7:00 pm	7:30 pm
8:00 pm	8:30 pm
9:00 pm	9:30 pm

DAY / DATE ______________________________

MY GOALS TODAY

____

____

____

____

____

____

NOTES

TIME BLOCKS

3:00 am	3:30 am
4:00 am	4:30 am
5:00 am	5:30 am
6:00 am	6:30 am
7:00 am	7:30 am
8:00 am	8:30 am
9:00 am	9:30 am
10:00 am	10:30 am
11:00 am	11:30 am
12:00 pm	12:30 pm
1:00 pm	1:30 pm
2:00 pm	2:30 pm
3:00 pm	3:30 pm
4:00 pm	4:30 pm
5:00 pm	5:30 pm
6:00 pm	6:30 pm
7:00 pm	7:30 pm
8:00 pm	8:30 pm
9:00 pm	9:30 pm

DAY / DATE ______________________________

MY GOALS TODAY

____

____

____

____

____

____

NOTES

TIME BLOCKS

3:00 am	3:30 am
4:00 am	4:30 am
5:00 am	5:30 am
6:00 am	6:30 am
7:00 am	7:30 am
8:00 am	8:30 am
9:00 am	9:30 am
10:00 am	10:30 am
11:00 am	11:30 am
12:00 pm	12:30 pm
1:00 pm	1:30 pm
2:00 pm	2:30 pm
3:00 pm	3:30 pm
4:00 pm	4:30 pm
5:00 pm	5:30 pm
6:00 pm	6:30 pm
7:00 pm	7:30 pm
8:00 pm	8:30 pm
9:00 pm	9:30 pm

DAY / DATE ______________________________

MY GOALS TODAY

____
____
____
____
____
____

NOTES

TIME BLOCKS

3:00 am	3:30 am
4:00 am	4:30 am
5:00 am	5:30 am
6:00 am	6:30 am
7:00 am	7:30 am
8:00 am	8:30 am
9:00 am	9:30 am
10:00 am	10:30 am
11:00 am	11:30 am
12:00 pm	12:30 pm
1:00 pm	1:30 pm
2:00 pm	2:30 pm
3:00 pm	3:30 pm
4:00 pm	4:30 pm
5:00 pm	5:30 pm
6:00 pm	6:30 pm
7:00 pm	7:30 pm
8:00 pm	8:30 pm
9:00 pm	9:30 pm

DAY / DATE ______________________________

MY GOALS TODAY

____
____
____
____
____
____

NOTES

TIME BLOCKS

3:00 am	3:30 am
4:00 am	4:30 am
5:00 am	5:30 am
6:00 am	6:30 am
7:00 am	7:30 am
8:00 am	8:30 am
9:00 am	9:30 am
10:00 am	10:30 am
11:00 am	11:30 am
12:00 pm	12:30 pm
1:00 pm	1:30 pm
2:00 pm	2:30 pm
3:00 pm	3:30 pm
4:00 pm	4:30 pm
5:00 pm	5:30 pm
6:00 pm	6:30 pm
7:00 pm	7:30 pm
8:00 pm	8:30 pm
9:00 pm	9:30 pm

DAY / DATE ______________________________

MY GOALS TODAY

____

____

____

____

____

____

NOTES

TIME BLOCKS

3:00 am	3:30 am
4:00 am	4:30 am
5:00 am	5:30 am
6:00 am	6:30 am
7:00 am	7:30 am
8:00 am	8:30 am
9:00 am	9:30 am
10:00 am	10:30 am
11:00 am	11:30 am
12:00 pm	12:30 pm
1:00 pm	1:30 pm
2:00 pm	2:30 pm
3:00 pm	3:30 pm
4:00 pm	4:30 pm
5:00 pm	5:30 pm
6:00 pm	6:30 pm
7:00 pm	7:30 pm
8:00 pm	8:30 pm
9:00 pm	9:30 pm

DAY / DATE ______________________________

MY GOALS TODAY

____

____

____

____

____

____

NOTES

TIME BLOCKS

3:00 am	3:30 am
4:00 am	4:30 am
5:00 am	5:30 am
6:00 am	6:30 am
7:00 am	7:30 am
8:00 am	8:30 am
9:00 am	9:30 am
10:00 am	10:30 am
11:00 am	11:30 am
12:00 pm	12:30 pm
1:00 pm	1:30 pm
2:00 pm	2:30 pm
3:00 pm	3:30 pm
4:00 pm	4:30 pm
5:00 pm	5:30 pm
6:00 pm	6:30 pm
7:00 pm	7:30 pm
8:00 pm	8:30 pm
9:00 pm	9:30 pm

DAY / DATE ______________________________

MY GOALS TODAY

____

____

____

____

____

____

NOTES

TIME BLOCKS

3:00 am	3:30 am
4:00 am	4:30 am
5:00 am	5:30 am
6:00 am	6:30 am
7:00 am	7:30 am
8:00 am	8:30 am
9:00 am	9:30 am
10:00 am	10:30 am
11:00 am	11:30 am
12:00 pm	12:30 pm
1:00 pm	1:30 pm
2:00 pm	2:30 pm
3:00 pm	3:30 pm
4:00 pm	4:30 pm
5:00 pm	5:30 pm
6:00 pm	6:30 pm
7:00 pm	7:30 pm
8:00 pm	8:30 pm
9:00 pm	9:30 pm

DAY / DATE ______________________________

MY GOALS TODAY

____

____

____

____

____

____

NOTES

TIME BLOCKS

3:00 am	3:30 am
4:00 am	4:30 am
5:00 am	5:30 am
6:00 am	6:30 am
7:00 am	7:30 am
8:00 am	8:30 am
9:00 am	9:30 am
10:00 am	10:30 am
11:00 am	11:30 am
12:00 pm	12:30 pm
1:00 pm	1:30 pm
2:00 pm	2:30 pm
3:00 pm	3:30 pm
4:00 pm	4:30 pm
5:00 pm	5:30 pm
6:00 pm	6:30 pm
7:00 pm	7:30 pm
8:00 pm	8:30 pm
9:00 pm	9:30 pm

DAY / DATE ______________________________

MY GOALS TODAY

____
____
____
____
____
____

NOTES

TIME BLOCKS

3:00 am	3:30 am
4:00 am	4:30 am
5:00 am	5:30 am
6:00 am	6:30 am
7:00 am	7:30 am
8:00 am	8:30 am
9:00 am	9:30 am
10:00 am	10:30 am
11:00 am	11:30 am
12:00 pm	12:30 pm
1:00 pm	1:30 pm
2:00 pm	2:30 pm
3:00 pm	3:30 pm
4:00 pm	4:30 pm
5:00 pm	5:30 pm
6:00 pm	6:30 pm
7:00 pm	7:30 pm
8:00 pm	8:30 pm
9:00 pm	9:30 pm

DAY / DATE ______________________

MY GOALS TODAY

____

____

____

____

____

____

NOTES

TIME BLOCKS

3:00 am	3:30 am
4:00 am	4:30 am
5:00 am	5:30 am
6:00 am	6:30 am
7:00 am	7:30 am
8:00 am	8:30 am
9:00 am	9:30 am
10:00 am	10:30 am
11:00 am	11:30 am
12:00 pm	12:30 pm
1:00 pm	1:30 pm
2:00 pm	2:30 pm
3:00 pm	3:30 pm
4:00 pm	4:30 pm
5:00 pm	5:30 pm
6:00 pm	6:30 pm
7:00 pm	7:30 pm
8:00 pm	8:30 pm
9:00 pm	9:30 pm

DAY / DATE ______________________________

MY GOALS TODAY

____
____
____
____
____
____

NOTES

TIME BLOCKS

3:00 am	3:30 am
4:00 am	4:30 am
5:00 am	5:30 am
6:00 am	6:30 am
7:00 am	7:30 am
8:00 am	8:30 am
9:00 am	9:30 am
10:00 am	10:30 am
11:00 am	11:30 am
12:00 pm	12:30 pm
1:00 pm	1:30 pm
2:00 pm	2:30 pm
3:00 pm	3:30 pm
4:00 pm	4:30 pm
5:00 pm	5:30 pm
6:00 pm	6:30 pm
7:00 pm	7:30 pm
8:00 pm	8:30 pm
9:00 pm	9:30 pm

DAY / DATE ______________________

MY GOALS TODAY

____
____
____
____
____
____

NOTES

TIME BLOCKS

3:00 am	3:30 am
4:00 am	4:30 am
5:00 am	5:30 am
6:00 am	6:30 am
7:00 am	7:30 am
8:00 am	8:30 am
9:00 am	9:30 am
10:00 am	10:30 am
11:00 am	11:30 am
12:00 pm	12:30 pm
1:00 pm	1:30 pm
2:00 pm	2:30 pm
3:00 pm	3:30 pm
4:00 pm	4:30 pm
5:00 pm	5:30 pm
6:00 pm	6:30 pm
7:00 pm	7:30 pm
8:00 pm	8:30 pm
9:00 pm	9:30 pm

DAY / DATE ______________________________

MY GOALS TODAY

____
____
____
____
____
____

NOTES

TIME BLOCKS

3:00 am	3:30 am
4:00 am	4:30 am
5:00 am	5:30 am
6:00 am	6:30 am
7:00 am	7:30 am
8:00 am	8:30 am
9:00 am	9:30 am
10:00 am	10:30 am
11:00 am	11:30 am
12:00 pm	12:30 pm
1:00 pm	1:30 pm
2:00 pm	2:30 pm
3:00 pm	3:30 pm
4:00 pm	4:30 pm
5:00 pm	5:30 pm
6:00 pm	6:30 pm
7:00 pm	7:30 pm
8:00 pm	8:30 pm
9:00 pm	9:30 pm

TIME MASTERY AND BLOCKER

DAY / DATE ______________________________

MY GOALS TODAY

____

____

____

____

____

____

NOTES

TIME BLOCKS

3:00 am	3:30 am
4:00 am	4:30 am
5:00 am	5:30 am
6:00 am	6:30 am
7:00 am	7:30 am
8:00 am	8:30 am
9:00 am	9:30 am
10:00 am	10:30 am
11:00 am	11:30 am
12:00 pm	12:30 pm
1:00 pm	1:30 pm
2:00 pm	2:30 pm
3:00 pm	3:30 pm
4:00 pm	4:30 pm
5:00 pm	5:30 pm
6:00 pm	6:30 pm
7:00 pm	7:30 pm
8:00 pm	8:30 pm
9:00 pm	9:30 pm

Thoughts become words. Words become action. Actions become character. Character becomes destiny.

DAY / DATE ______________________________

MY GOALS TODAY

____
____
____
____
____
____

NOTES

TIME BLOCKS

3:00 am	3:30 am
4:00 am	4:30 am
5:00 am	5:30 am
6:00 am	6:30 am
7:00 am	7:30 am
8:00 am	8:30 am
9:00 am	9:30 am
10:00 am	10:30 am
11:00 am	11:30 am
12:00 pm	12:30 pm
1:00 pm	1:30 pm
2:00 pm	2:30 pm
3:00 pm	3:30 pm
4:00 pm	4:30 pm
5:00 pm	5:30 pm
6:00 pm	6:30 pm
7:00 pm	7:30 pm
8:00 pm	8:30 pm
9:00 pm	9:30 pm

DAY / DATE ______________________________

MY GOALS TODAY

____

____

____

____

____

____

NOTES

TIME BLOCKS

3:00 am	3:30 am
4:00 am	4:30 am
5:00 am	5:30 am
6:00 am	6:30 am
7:00 am	7:30 am
8:00 am	8:30 am
9:00 am	9:30 am
10:00 am	10:30 am
11:00 am	11:30 am
12:00 pm	12:30 pm
1:00 pm	1:30 pm
2:00 pm	2:30 pm
3:00 pm	3:30 pm
4:00 pm	4:30 pm
5:00 pm	5:30 pm
6:00 pm	6:30 pm
7:00 pm	7:30 pm
8:00 pm	8:30 pm
9:00 pm	9:30 pm

DAY / DATE ______________________________

MY GOALS TODAY

____

____

____

____

____

____

NOTES

TIME BLOCKS

3:00 am	3:30 am
4:00 am	4:30 am
5:00 am	5:30 am
6:00 am	6:30 am
7:00 am	7:30 am
8:00 am	8:30 am
9:00 am	9:30 am
10:00 am	10:30 am
11:00 am	11:30 am
12:00 pm	12:30 pm
1:00 pm	1:30 pm
2:00 pm	2:30 pm
3:00 pm	3:30 pm
4:00 pm	4:30 pm
5:00 pm	5:30 pm
6:00 pm	6:30 pm
7:00 pm	7:30 pm
8:00 pm	8:30 pm
9:00 pm	9:30 pm

DAY / DATE ______________________________

MY GOALS TODAY

____

____

____

____

____

____

TIME BLOCKS

3:00 am	3:30 am
4:00 am	4:30 am
5:00 am	5:30 am
6:00 am	6:30 am
7:00 am	7:30 am
8:00 am	8:30 am
9:00 am	9:30 am
10:00 am	10:30 am
11:00 am	11:30 am
12:00 pm	12:30 pm
1:00 pm	1:30 pm
2:00 pm	2:30 pm
3:00 pm	3:30 pm
4:00 pm	4:30 pm
5:00 pm	5:30 pm
6:00 pm	6:30 pm
7:00 pm	7:30 pm
8:00 pm	8:30 pm
9:00 pm	9:30 pm

NOTES

Thoughts become words. Words become action. Actions become character. Character becomes destiny.

DAY / DATE ____________________

MY GOALS TODAY

NOTES

TIME BLOCKS

3:00 am	3:30 am
4:00 am	4:30 am
5:00 am	5:30 am
6:00 am	6:30 am
7:00 am	7:30 am
8:00 am	8:30 am
9:00 am	9:30 am
10:00 am	10:30 am
11:00 am	11:30 am
12:00 pm	12:30 pm
1:00 pm	1:30 pm
2:00 pm	2:30 pm
3:00 pm	3:30 pm
4:00 pm	4:30 pm
5:00 pm	5:30 pm
6:00 pm	6:30 pm
7:00 pm	7:30 pm
8:00 pm	8:30 pm
9:00 pm	9:30 pm

DAY / DATE ______________________________

MY GOALS TODAY

____
____
____
____
____
____

NOTES

TIME BLOCKS

3:00 am	3:30 am
4:00 am	4:30 am
5:00 am	5:30 am
6:00 am	6:30 am
7:00 am	7:30 am
8:00 am	8:30 am
9:00 am	9:30 am
10:00 am	10:30 am
11:00 am	11:30 am
12:00 pm	12:30 pm
1:00 pm	1:30 pm
2:00 pm	2:30 pm
3:00 pm	3:30 pm
4:00 pm	4:30 pm
5:00 pm	5:30 pm
6:00 pm	6:30 pm
7:00 pm	7:30 pm
8:00 pm	8:30 pm
9:00 pm	9:30 pm

DAY / DATE ______________________________

MY GOALS TODAY

____
____
____
____
____
____

NOTES

TIME BLOCKS

3:00 am	3:30 am
4:00 am	4:30 am
5:00 am	5:30 am
6:00 am	6:30 am
7:00 am	7:30 am
8:00 am	8:30 am
9:00 am	9:30 am
10:00 am	10:30 am
11:00 am	11:30 am
12:00 pm	12:30 pm
1:00 pm	1:30 pm
2:00 pm	2:30 pm
3:00 pm	3:30 pm
4:00 pm	4:30 pm
5:00 pm	5:30 pm
6:00 pm	6:30 pm
7:00 pm	7:30 pm
8:00 pm	8:30 pm
9:00 pm	9:30 pm

DAY / DATE ______________________________

MY GOALS TODAY

____

____

____

____

____

____

NOTES

TIME BLOCKS

3:00 am	3:30 am
4:00 am	4:30 am
5:00 am	5:30 am
6:00 am	6:30 am
7:00 am	7:30 am
8:00 am	8:30 am
9:00 am	9:30 am
10:00 am	10:30 am
11:00 am	11:30 am
12:00 pm	12:30 pm
1:00 pm	1:30 pm
2:00 pm	2:30 pm
3:00 pm	3:30 pm
4:00 pm	4:30 pm
5:00 pm	5:30 pm
6:00 pm	6:30 pm
7:00 pm	7:30 pm
8:00 pm	8:30 pm
9:00 pm	9:30 pm

DAY / DATE ____

MY GOALS TODAY

____
____
____
____
____
____

NOTES

TIME BLOCKS

3:00 am	3:30 am
4:00 am	4:30 am
5:00 am	5:30 am
6:00 am	6:30 am
7:00 am	7:30 am
8:00 am	8:30 am
9:00 am	9:30 am
10:00 am	10:30 am
11:00 am	11:30 am
12:00 pm	12:30 pm
1:00 pm	1:30 pm
2:00 pm	2:30 pm
3:00 pm	3:30 pm
4:00 pm	4:30 pm
5:00 pm	5:30 pm
6:00 pm	6:30 pm
7:00 pm	7:30 pm
8:00 pm	8:30 pm
9:00 pm	9:30 pm

DAY / DATE ______________________________

MY GOALS TODAY

____

____

____

____

____

____

NOTES

TIME BLOCKS

3:00 am	3:30 am
4:00 am	4:30 am
5:00 am	5:30 am
6:00 am	6:30 am
7:00 am	7:30 am
8:00 am	8:30 am
9:00 am	9:30 am
10:00 am	10:30 am
11:00 am	11:30 am
12:00 pm	12:30 pm
1:00 pm	1:30 pm
2:00 pm	2:30 pm
3:00 pm	3:30 pm
4:00 pm	4:30 pm
5:00 pm	5:30 pm
6:00 pm	6:30 pm
7:00 pm	7:30 pm
8:00 pm	8:30 pm
9:00 pm	9:30 pm

DAY / DATE ______________________________

MY GOALS TODAY

____

____

____

____

____

____

NOTES

TIME BLOCKS

3:00 am	3:30 am
4:00 am	4:30 am
5:00 am	5:30 am
6:00 am	6:30 am
7:00 am	7:30 am
8:00 am	8:30 am
9:00 am	9:30 am
10:00 am	10:30 am
11:00 am	11:30 am
12:00 pm	12:30 pm
1:00 pm	1:30 pm
2:00 pm	2:30 pm
3:00 pm	3:30 pm
4:00 pm	4:30 pm
5:00 pm	5:30 pm
6:00 pm	6:30 pm
7:00 pm	7:30 pm
8:00 pm	8:30 pm
9:00 pm	9:30 pm

DAY / DATE ______________________________

MY GOALS TODAY

____

____

____

____

____

____

NOTES

TIME BLOCKS

3:00 am	3:30 am
4:00 am	4:30 am
5:00 am	5:30 am
6:00 am	6:30 am
7:00 am	7:30 am
8:00 am	8:30 am
9:00 am	9:30 am
10:00 am	10:30 am
11:00 am	11:30 am
12:00 pm	12:30 pm
1:00 pm	1:30 pm
2:00 pm	2:30 pm
3:00 pm	3:30 pm
4:00 pm	4:30 pm
5:00 pm	5:30 pm
6:00 pm	6:30 pm
7:00 pm	7:30 pm
8:00 pm	8:30 pm
9:00 pm	9:30 pm

DAY / DATE ______________________________

MY GOALS TODAY

____

____

____

____

____

____

NOTES

TIME BLOCKS

3:00 am	3:30 am
4:00 am	4:30 am
5:00 am	5:30 am
6:00 am	6:30 am
7:00 am	7:30 am
8:00 am	8:30 am
9:00 am	9:30 am
10:00 am	10:30 am
11:00 am	11:30 am
12:00 pm	12:30 pm
1:00 pm	1:30 pm
2:00 pm	2:30 pm
3:00 pm	3:30 pm
4:00 pm	4:30 pm
5:00 pm	5:30 pm
6:00 pm	6:30 pm
7:00 pm	7:30 pm
8:00 pm	8:30 pm
9:00 pm	9:30 pm

DAY / DATE ______________________________

MY GOALS TODAY

____

____

____

____

____

____

NOTES

TIME BLOCKS

3:00 am	3:30 am
4:00 am	4:30 am
5:00 am	5:30 am
6:00 am	6:30 am
7:00 am	7:30 am
8:00 am	8:30 am
9:00 am	9:30 am
10:00 am	10:30 am
11:00 am	11:30 am
12:00 pm	12:30 pm
1:00 pm	1:30 pm
2:00 pm	2:30 pm
3:00 pm	3:30 pm
4:00 pm	4:30 pm
5:00 pm	5:30 pm
6:00 pm	6:30 pm
7:00 pm	7:30 pm
8:00 pm	8:30 pm
9:00 pm	9:30 pm

DAY / DATE ____________________

MY GOALS TODAY

____

____

____

____

____

____

NOTES

TIME BLOCKS

3:00 am	3:30 am
4:00 am	4:30 am
5:00 am	5:30 am
6:00 am	6:30 am
7:00 am	7:30 am
8:00 am	8:30 am
9:00 am	9:30 am
10:00 am	10:30 am
11:00 am	11:30 am
12:00 pm	12:30 pm
1:00 pm	1:30 pm
2:00 pm	2:30 pm
3:00 pm	3:30 pm
4:00 pm	4:30 pm
5:00 pm	5:30 pm
6:00 pm	6:30 pm
7:00 pm	7:30 pm
8:00 pm	8:30 pm
9:00 pm	9:30 pm

DAY / DATE ____________________

MY GOALS TODAY

____

____

____

____

____

____

NOTES

TIME BLOCKS

3:00 am	3:30 am
4:00 am	4:30 am
5:00 am	5:30 am
6:00 am	6:30 am
7:00 am	7:30 am
8:00 am	8:30 am
9:00 am	9:30 am
10:00 am	10:30 am
11:00 am	11:30 am
12:00 pm	12:30 pm
1:00 pm	1:30 pm
2:00 pm	2:30 pm
3:00 pm	3:30 pm
4:00 pm	4:30 pm
5:00 pm	5:30 pm
6:00 pm	6:30 pm
7:00 pm	7:30 pm
8:00 pm	8:30 pm
9:00 pm	9:30 pm

DAY / DATE ______________________________

MY GOALS TODAY

____

____

____

____

____

____

NOTES

TIME BLOCKS

3:00 am	3:30 am
4:00 am	4:30 am
5:00 am	5:30 am
6:00 am	6:30 am
7:00 am	7:30 am
8:00 am	8:30 am
9:00 am	9:30 am
10:00 am	10:30 am
11:00 am	11:30 am
12:00 pm	12:30 pm
1:00 pm	1:30 pm
2:00 pm	2:30 pm
3:00 pm	3:30 pm
4:00 pm	4:30 pm
5:00 pm	5:30 pm
6:00 pm	6:30 pm
7:00 pm	7:30 pm
8:00 pm	8:30 pm
9:00 pm	9:30 pm

DAY / DATE ____________________

MY GOALS TODAY

____

____

____

____

____

____

NOTES

TIME BLOCKS

3:00 am	3:30 am
4:00 am	4:30 am
5:00 am	5:30 am
6:00 am	6:30 am
7:00 am	7:30 am
8:00 am	8:30 am
9:00 am	9:30 am
10:00 am	10:30 am
11:00 am	11:30 am
12:00 pm	12:30 pm
1:00 pm	1:30 pm
2:00 pm	2:30 pm
3:00 pm	3:30 pm
4:00 pm	4:30 pm
5:00 pm	5:30 pm
6:00 pm	6:30 pm
7:00 pm	7:30 pm
8:00 pm	8:30 pm
9:00 pm	9:30 pm

DAY / DATE ______________________________

MY GOALS TODAY

____
____
____
____
____
____

NOTES

TIME BLOCKS

3:00 am	3:30 am
4:00 am	4:30 am
5:00 am	5:30 am
6:00 am	6:30 am
7:00 am	7:30 am
8:00 am	8:30 am
9:00 am	9:30 am
10:00 am	10:30 am
11:00 am	11:30 am
12:00 pm	12:30 pm
1:00 pm	1:30 pm
2:00 pm	2:30 pm
3:00 pm	3:30 pm
4:00 pm	4:30 pm
5:00 pm	5:30 pm
6:00 pm	6:30 pm
7:00 pm	7:30 pm
8:00 pm	8:30 pm
9:00 pm	9:30 pm

Thoughts become words. Words become action. Actions become character. Character becomes destiny.

DAY / DATE ______________________________

MY GOALS TODAY

____

____

____

____

____

____

NOTES

TIME BLOCKS

3:00 am	3:30 am
4:00 am	4:30 am
5:00 am	5:30 am
6:00 am	6:30 am
7:00 am	7:30 am
8:00 am	8:30 am
9:00 am	9:30 am
10:00 am	10:30 am
11:00 am	11:30 am
12:00 pm	12:30 pm
1:00 pm	1:30 pm
2:00 pm	2:30 pm
3:00 pm	3:30 pm
4:00 pm	4:30 pm
5:00 pm	5:30 pm
6:00 pm	6:30 pm
7:00 pm	7:30 pm
8:00 pm	8:30 pm
9:00 pm	9:30 pm

DAY / DATE ____________________

MY GOALS TODAY

NOTES

TIME BLOCKS

3:00 am	3:30 am
4:00 am	4:30 am
5:00 am	5:30 am
6:00 am	6:30 am
7:00 am	7:30 am
8:00 am	8:30 am
9:00 am	9:30 am
10:00 am	10:30 am
11:00 am	11:30 am
12:00 pm	12:30 pm
1:00 pm	1:30 pm
2:00 pm	2:30 pm
3:00 pm	3:30 pm
4:00 pm	4:30 pm
5:00 pm	5:30 pm
6:00 pm	6:30 pm
7:00 pm	7:30 pm
8:00 pm	8:30 pm
9:00 pm	9:30 pm

DAY / DATE ______________________________

MY GOALS TODAY

____

____

____

____

____

____

NOTES

TIME BLOCKS

3:00 am	3:30 am
4:00 am	4:30 am
5:00 am	5:30 am
6:00 am	6:30 am
7:00 am	7:30 am
8:00 am	8:30 am
9:00 am	9:30 am
10:00 am	10:30 am
11:00 am	11:30 am
12:00 pm	12:30 pm
1:00 pm	1:30 pm
2:00 pm	2:30 pm
3:00 pm	3:30 pm
4:00 pm	4:30 pm
5:00 pm	5:30 pm
6:00 pm	6:30 pm
7:00 pm	7:30 pm
8:00 pm	8:30 pm
9:00 pm	9:30 pm

DAY / DATE ______________________________

MY GOALS TODAY

____

____

____

____

____

____

NOTES

TIME BLOCKS

3:00 am	3:30 am
4:00 am	4:30 am
5:00 am	5:30 am
6:00 am	6:30 am
7:00 am	7:30 am
8:00 am	8:30 am
9:00 am	9:30 am
10:00 am	10:30 am
11:00 am	11:30 am
12:00 pm	12:30 pm
1:00 pm	1:30 pm
2:00 pm	2:30 pm
3:00 pm	3:30 pm
4:00 pm	4:30 pm
5:00 pm	5:30 pm
6:00 pm	6:30 pm
7:00 pm	7:30 pm
8:00 pm	8:30 pm
9:00 pm	9:30 pm

TIME MASTERY AND BLOCKER

DAY / DATE ______________________________

MY GOALS TODAY

____

____

____

____

____

____

NOTES

TIME BLOCKS

3:00 am	3:30 am
4:00 am	4:30 am
5:00 am	5:30 am
6:00 am	6:30 am
7:00 am	7:30 am
8:00 am	8:30 am
9:00 am	9:30 am
10:00 am	10:30 am
11:00 am	11:30 am
12:00 pm	12:30 pm
1:00 pm	1:30 pm
2:00 pm	2:30 pm
3:00 pm	3:30 pm
4:00 pm	4:30 pm
5:00 pm	5:30 pm
6:00 pm	6:30 pm
7:00 pm	7:30 pm
8:00 pm	8:30 pm
9:00 pm	9:30 pm

DAY / DATE ______________________________

MY GOALS TODAY

____
____
____
____
____
____

NOTES

TIME BLOCKS

3:00 am	3:30 am
4:00 am	4:30 am
5:00 am	5:30 am
6:00 am	6:30 am
7:00 am	7:30 am
8:00 am	8:30 am
9:00 am	9:30 am
10:00 am	10:30 am
11:00 am	11:30 am
12:00 pm	12:30 pm
1:00 pm	1:30 pm
2:00 pm	2:30 pm
3:00 pm	3:30 pm
4:00 pm	4:30 pm
5:00 pm	5:30 pm
6:00 pm	6:30 pm
7:00 pm	7:30 pm
8:00 pm	8:30 pm
9:00 pm	9:30 pm

DAY / DATE ____________________

MY GOALS TODAY

____

____

____

____

____

____

NOTES

TIME BLOCKS

3:00 am	3:30 am
4:00 am	4:30 am
5:00 am	5:30 am
6:00 am	6:30 am
7:00 am	7:30 am
8:00 am	8:30 am
9:00 am	9:30 am
10:00 am	10:30 am
11:00 am	11:30 am
12:00 pm	12:30 pm
1:00 pm	1:30 pm
2:00 pm	2:30 pm
3:00 pm	3:30 pm
4:00 pm	4:30 pm
5:00 pm	5:30 pm
6:00 pm	6:30 pm
7:00 pm	7:30 pm
8:00 pm	8:30 pm
9:00 pm	9:30 pm

DAY / DATE ______________________________

MY GOALS TODAY

____

____

____

____

____

____

NOTES

TIME BLOCKS

3:00 am	3:30 am
4:00 am	4:30 am
5:00 am	5:30 am
6:00 am	6:30 am
7:00 am	7:30 am
8:00 am	8:30 am
9:00 am	9:30 am
10:00 am	10:30 am
11:00 am	11:30 am
12:00 pm	12:30 pm
1:00 pm	1:30 pm
2:00 pm	2:30 pm
3:00 pm	3:30 pm
4:00 pm	4:30 pm
5:00 pm	5:30 pm
6:00 pm	6:30 pm
7:00 pm	7:30 pm
8:00 pm	8:30 pm
9:00 pm	9:30 pm

DAY / DATE ______________________________

MY GOALS TODAY

____

____

____

____

____

____

NOTES

TIME BLOCKS

3:00 am	3:30 am
4:00 am	4:30 am
5:00 am	5:30 am
6:00 am	6:30 am
7:00 am	7:30 am
8:00 am	8:30 am
9:00 am	9:30 am
10:00 am	10:30 am
11:00 am	11:30 am
12:00 pm	12:30 pm
1:00 pm	1:30 pm
2:00 pm	2:30 pm
3:00 pm	3:30 pm
4:00 pm	4:30 pm
5:00 pm	5:30 pm
6:00 pm	6:30 pm
7:00 pm	7:30 pm
8:00 pm	8:30 pm
9:00 pm	9:30 pm

DAY / DATE ______________________________

MY GOALS TODAY

____
____
____
____
____
____

NOTES

TIME BLOCKS

3:00 am	3:30 am
4:00 am	4:30 am
5:00 am	5:30 am
6:00 am	6:30 am
7:00 am	7:30 am
8:00 am	8:30 am
9:00 am	9:30 am
10:00 am	10:30 am
11:00 am	11:30 am
12:00 pm	12:30 pm
1:00 pm	1:30 pm
2:00 pm	2:30 pm
3:00 pm	3:30 pm
4:00 pm	4:30 pm
5:00 pm	5:30 pm
6:00 pm	6:30 pm
7:00 pm	7:30 pm
8:00 pm	8:30 pm
9:00 pm	9:30 pm

DAY / DATE ______________________________

MY GOALS TODAY

____

____

____

____

____

____

NOTES

TIME BLOCKS

3:00 am	3:30 am
4:00 am	4:30 am
5:00 am	5:30 am
6:00 am	6:30 am
7:00 am	7:30 am
8:00 am	8:30 am
9:00 am	9:30 am
10:00 am	10:30 am
11:00 am	11:30 am
12:00 pm	12:30 pm
1:00 pm	1:30 pm
2:00 pm	2:30 pm
3:00 pm	3:30 pm
4:00 pm	4:30 pm
5:00 pm	5:30 pm
6:00 pm	6:30 pm
7:00 pm	7:30 pm
8:00 pm	8:30 pm
9:00 pm	9:30 pm

DAY / DATE ______________________________

MY GOALS TODAY

____

____

____

____

____

____

NOTES

TIME BLOCKS

3:00 am	3:30 am
4:00 am	4:30 am
5:00 am	5:30 am
6:00 am	6:30 am
7:00 am	7:30 am
8:00 am	8:30 am
9:00 am	9:30 am
10:00 am	10:30 am
11:00 am	11:30 am
12:00 pm	12:30 pm
1:00 pm	1:30 pm
2:00 pm	2:30 pm
3:00 pm	3:30 pm
4:00 pm	4:30 pm
5:00 pm	5:30 pm
6:00 pm	6:30 pm
7:00 pm	7:30 pm
8:00 pm	8:30 pm
9:00 pm	9:30 pm

TIME MASTERY AND BLOCKER

DAY / DATE ______________________________

MY GOALS TODAY

____

____

____

____

____

____

NOTES

TIME BLOCKS

3:00 am	3:30 am
4:00 am	4:30 am
5:00 am	5:30 am
6:00 am	6:30 am
7:00 am	7:30 am
8:00 am	8:30 am
9:00 am	9:30 am
10:00 am	10:30 am
11:00 am	11:30 am
12:00 pm	12:30 pm
1:00 pm	1:30 pm
2:00 pm	2:30 pm
3:00 pm	3:30 pm
4:00 pm	4:30 pm
5:00 pm	5:30 pm
6:00 pm	6:30 pm
7:00 pm	7:30 pm
8:00 pm	8:30 pm
9:00 pm	9:30 pm

Thoughts become words. Words become action. Actions become character. Character becomes destiny.

DAY / DATE ______________________________

MY GOALS TODAY

____

____

____

____

____

____

NOTES

TIME BLOCKS

3:00 am	3:30 am
4:00 am	4:30 am
5:00 am	5:30 am
6:00 am	6:30 am
7:00 am	7:30 am
8:00 am	8:30 am
9:00 am	9:30 am
10:00 am	10:30 am
11:00 am	11:30 am
12:00 pm	12:30 pm
1:00 pm	1:30 pm
2:00 pm	2:30 pm
3:00 pm	3:30 pm
4:00 pm	4:30 pm
5:00 pm	5:30 pm
6:00 pm	6:30 pm
7:00 pm	7:30 pm
8:00 pm	8:30 pm
9:00 pm	9:30 pm

DAY / DATE ______________________________

MY GOALS TODAY

____

____

____

____

____

____

NOTES

TIME BLOCKS

3:00 am	3:30 am
4:00 am	4:30 am
5:00 am	5:30 am
6:00 am	6:30 am
7:00 am	7:30 am
8:00 am	8:30 am
9:00 am	9:30 am
10:00 am	10:30 am
11:00 am	11:30 am
12:00 pm	12:30 pm
1:00 pm	1:30 pm
2:00 pm	2:30 pm
3:00 pm	3:30 pm
4:00 pm	4:30 pm
5:00 pm	5:30 pm
6:00 pm	6:30 pm
7:00 pm	7:30 pm
8:00 pm	8:30 pm
9:00 pm	9:30 pm

DAY / DATE ____________________

MY GOALS TODAY

____

____

____

____

____

____

NOTES

TIME BLOCKS

3:00 am	3:30 am
4:00 am	4:30 am
5:00 am	5:30 am
6:00 am	6:30 am
7:00 am	7:30 am
8:00 am	8:30 am
9:00 am	9:30 am
10:00 am	10:30 am
11:00 am	11:30 am
12:00 pm	12:30 pm
1:00 pm	1:30 pm
2:00 pm	2:30 pm
3:00 pm	3:30 pm
4:00 pm	4:30 pm
5:00 pm	5:30 pm
6:00 pm	6:30 pm
7:00 pm	7:30 pm
8:00 pm	8:30 pm
9:00 pm	9:30 pm

DAY / DATE ______________________________

MY GOALS TODAY

____

____

____

____

____

____

NOTES

TIME BLOCKS

3:00 am	3:30 am
4:00 am	4:30 am
5:00 am	5:30 am
6:00 am	6:30 am
7:00 am	7:30 am
8:00 am	8:30 am
9:00 am	9:30 am
10:00 am	10:30 am
11:00 am	11:30 am
12:00 pm	12:30 pm
1:00 pm	1:30 pm
2:00 pm	2:30 pm
3:00 pm	3:30 pm
4:00 pm	4:30 pm
5:00 pm	5:30 pm
6:00 pm	6:30 pm
7:00 pm	7:30 pm
8:00 pm	8:30 pm
9:00 pm	9:30 pm

DAY / DATE ____________________

MY GOALS TODAY

NOTES

TIME BLOCKS

3:00 am	3:30 am
4:00 am	4:30 am
5:00 am	5:30 am
6:00 am	6:30 am
7:00 am	7:30 am
8:00 am	8:30 am
9:00 am	9:30 am
10:00 am	10:30 am
11:00 am	11:30 am
12:00 pm	12:30 pm
1:00 pm	1:30 pm
2:00 pm	2:30 pm
3:00 pm	3:30 pm
4:00 pm	4:30 pm
5:00 pm	5:30 pm
6:00 pm	6:30 pm
7:00 pm	7:30 pm
8:00 pm	8:30 pm
9:00 pm	9:30 pm

DAY / DATE ______________________________

MY GOALS TODAY

____

____

____

____

____

____

NOTES

TIME BLOCKS

3:00 am	3:30 am
4:00 am	4:30 am
5:00 am	5:30 am
6:00 am	6:30 am
7:00 am	7:30 am
8:00 am	8:30 am
9:00 am	9:30 am
10:00 am	10:30 am
11:00 am	11:30 am
12:00 pm	12:30 pm
1:00 pm	1:30 pm
2:00 pm	2:30 pm
3:00 pm	3:30 pm
4:00 pm	4:30 pm
5:00 pm	5:30 pm
6:00 pm	6:30 pm
7:00 pm	7:30 pm
8:00 pm	8:30 pm
9:00 pm	9:30 pm

DAY / DATE ______________________________

MY GOALS TODAY

____

____

____

____

____

____

NOTES

TIME BLOCKS

3:00 am	3:30 am
4:00 am	4:30 am
5:00 am	5:30 am
6:00 am	6:30 am
7:00 am	7:30 am
8:00 am	8:30 am
9:00 am	9:30 am
10:00 am	10:30 am
11:00 am	11:30 am
12:00 pm	12:30 pm
1:00 pm	1:30 pm
2:00 pm	2:30 pm
3:00 pm	3:30 pm
4:00 pm	4:30 pm
5:00 pm	5:30 pm
6:00 pm	6:30 pm
7:00 pm	7:30 pm
8:00 pm	8:30 pm
9:00 pm	9:30 pm

DAY / DATE ______________________________

MY GOALS TODAY

____
____
____
____
____
____

NOTES

TIME BLOCKS

3:00 am	3:30 am
4:00 am	4:30 am
5:00 am	5:30 am
6:00 am	6:30 am
7:00 am	7:30 am
8:00 am	8:30 am
9:00 am	9:30 am
10:00 am	10:30 am
11:00 am	11:30 am
12:00 pm	12:30 pm
1:00 pm	1:30 pm
2:00 pm	2:30 pm
3:00 pm	3:30 pm
4:00 pm	4:30 pm
5:00 pm	5:30 pm
6:00 pm	6:30 pm
7:00 pm	7:30 pm
8:00 pm	8:30 pm
9:00 pm	9:30 pm

DAY / DATE ______________________________

MY GOALS TODAY

____
____
____
____
____
____

NOTES

TIME BLOCKS

3:00 am	3:30 am
4:00 am	4:30 am
5:00 am	5:30 am
6:00 am	6:30 am
7:00 am	7:30 am
8:00 am	8:30 am
9:00 am	9:30 am
10:00 am	10:30 am
11:00 am	11:30 am
12:00 pm	12:30 pm
1:00 pm	1:30 pm
2:00 pm	2:30 pm
3:00 pm	3:30 pm
4:00 pm	4:30 pm
5:00 pm	5:30 pm
6:00 pm	6:30 pm
7:00 pm	7:30 pm
8:00 pm	8:30 pm
9:00 pm	9:30 pm

DAY / DATE ______________________________

MY GOALS TODAY

____

____

____

____

____

____

NOTES

TIME BLOCKS

3:00 am	3:30 am
4:00 am	4:30 am
5:00 am	5:30 am
6:00 am	6:30 am
7:00 am	7:30 am
8:00 am	8:30 am
9:00 am	9:30 am
10:00 am	10:30 am
11:00 am	11:30 am
12:00 pm	12:30 pm
1:00 pm	1:30 pm
2:00 pm	2:30 pm
3:00 pm	3:30 pm
4:00 pm	4:30 pm
5:00 pm	5:30 pm
6:00 pm	6:30 pm
7:00 pm	7:30 pm
8:00 pm	8:30 pm
9:00 pm	9:30 pm

DAY / DATE ______________________________

MY GOALS TODAY

____
____
____
____
____
____

NOTES

TIME BLOCKS

3:00 am	3:30 am
4:00 am	4:30 am
5:00 am	5:30 am
6:00 am	6:30 am
7:00 am	7:30 am
8:00 am	8:30 am
9:00 am	9:30 am
10:00 am	10:30 am
11:00 am	11:30 am
12:00 pm	12:30 pm
1:00 pm	1:30 pm
2:00 pm	2:30 pm
3:00 pm	3:30 pm
4:00 pm	4:30 pm
5:00 pm	5:30 pm
6:00 pm	6:30 pm
7:00 pm	7:30 pm
8:00 pm	8:30 pm
9:00 pm	9:30 pm

DAY / DATE ______________________________

MY GOALS TODAY

____
____
____
____
____
____

NOTES

TIME BLOCKS

3:00 am	3:30 am
4:00 am	4:30 am
5:00 am	5:30 am
6:00 am	6:30 am
7:00 am	7:30 am
8:00 am	8:30 am
9:00 am	9:30 am
10:00 am	10:30 am
11:00 am	11:30 am
12:00 pm	12:30 pm
1:00 pm	1:30 pm
2:00 pm	2:30 pm
3:00 pm	3:30 pm
4:00 pm	4:30 pm
5:00 pm	5:30 pm
6:00 pm	6:30 pm
7:00 pm	7:30 pm
8:00 pm	8:30 pm
9:00 pm	9:30 pm

Thoughts become words. Words become action. Actions become character. Character becomes destiny.

DAY / DATE ______________________________

MY GOALS TODAY

____

____

____

____

____

____

NOTES

TIME BLOCKS

3:00 am	3:30 am
4:00 am	4:30 am
5:00 am	5:30 am
6:00 am	6:30 am
7:00 am	7:30 am
8:00 am	8:30 am
9:00 am	9:30 am
10:00 am	10:30 am
11:00 am	11:30 am
12:00 pm	12:30 pm
1:00 pm	1:30 pm
2:00 pm	2:30 pm
3:00 pm	3:30 pm
4:00 pm	4:30 pm
5:00 pm	5:30 pm
6:00 pm	6:30 pm
7:00 pm	7:30 pm
8:00 pm	8:30 pm
9:00 pm	9:30 pm

DAY / DATE ______________________________

MY GOALS TODAY

____
____
____
____
____
____

NOTES

TIME BLOCKS

3:00 am	3:30 am
4:00 am	4:30 am
5:00 am	5:30 am
6:00 am	6:30 am
7:00 am	7:30 am
8:00 am	8:30 am
9:00 am	9:30 am
10:00 am	10:30 am
11:00 am	11:30 am
12:00 pm	12:30 pm
1:00 pm	1:30 pm
2:00 pm	2:30 pm
3:00 pm	3:30 pm
4:00 pm	4:30 pm
5:00 pm	5:30 pm
6:00 pm	6:30 pm
7:00 pm	7:30 pm
8:00 pm	8:30 pm
9:00 pm	9:30 pm

DAY / DATE ____________________

MY GOALS TODAY

____

____

____

____

____

____

NOTES

TIME BLOCKS

3:00 am	3:30 am
4:00 am	4:30 am
5:00 am	5:30 am
6:00 am	6:30 am
7:00 am	7:30 am
8:00 am	8:30 am
9:00 am	9:30 am
10:00 am	10:30 am
11:00 am	11:30 am
12:00 pm	12:30 pm
1:00 pm	1:30 pm
2:00 pm	2:30 pm
3:00 pm	3:30 pm
4:00 pm	4:30 pm
5:00 pm	5:30 pm
6:00 pm	6:30 pm
7:00 pm	7:30 pm
8:00 pm	8:30 pm
9:00 pm	9:30 pm

DAY / DATE ____________________

MY GOALS TODAY

____

____

____

____

____

____

NOTES

TIME BLOCKS

3:00 am	3:30 am
4:00 am	4:30 am
5:00 am	5:30 am
6:00 am	6:30 am
7:00 am	7:30 am
8:00 am	8:30 am
9:00 am	9:30 am
10:00 am	10:30 am
11:00 am	11:30 am
12:00 pm	12:30 pm
1:00 pm	1:30 pm
2:00 pm	2:30 pm
3:00 pm	3:30 pm
4:00 pm	4:30 pm
5:00 pm	5:30 pm
6:00 pm	6:30 pm
7:00 pm	7:30 pm
8:00 pm	8:30 pm
9:00 pm	9:30 pm

DAY / DATE ______________________________

MY GOALS TODAY

____

____

____

____

____

____

NOTES

TIME BLOCKS

3:00 am	3:30 am
4:00 am	4:30 am
5:00 am	5:30 am
6:00 am	6:30 am
7:00 am	7:30 am
8:00 am	8:30 am
9:00 am	9:30 am
10:00 am	10:30 am
11:00 am	11:30 am
12:00 pm	12:30 pm
1:00 pm	1:30 pm
2:00 pm	2:30 pm
3:00 pm	3:30 pm
4:00 pm	4:30 pm
5:00 pm	5:30 pm
6:00 pm	6:30 pm
7:00 pm	7:30 pm
8:00 pm	8:30 pm
9:00 pm	9:30 pm

DAY / DATE ______________________________

MY GOALS TODAY

____

____

____

____

____

____

NOTES

TIME BLOCKS

3:00 am	3:30 am
4:00 am	4:30 am
5:00 am	5:30 am
6:00 am	6:30 am
7:00 am	7:30 am
8:00 am	8:30 am
9:00 am	9:30 am
10:00 am	10:30 am
11:00 am	11:30 am
12:00 pm	12:30 pm
1:00 pm	1:30 pm
2:00 pm	2:30 pm
3:00 pm	3:30 pm
4:00 pm	4:30 pm
5:00 pm	5:30 pm
6:00 pm	6:30 pm
7:00 pm	7:30 pm
8:00 pm	8:30 pm
9:00 pm	9:30 pm

DAY / DATE ______________________________

MY GOALS TODAY

____

____

____

____

____

____

NOTES

TIME BLOCKS

3:00 am	3:30 am
4:00 am	4:30 am
5:00 am	5:30 am
6:00 am	6:30 am
7:00 am	7:30 am
8:00 am	8:30 am
9:00 am	9:30 am
10:00 am	10:30 am
11:00 am	11:30 am
12:00 pm	12:30 pm
1:00 pm	1:30 pm
2:00 pm	2:30 pm
3:00 pm	3:30 pm
4:00 pm	4:30 pm
5:00 pm	5:30 pm
6:00 pm	6:30 pm
7:00 pm	7:30 pm
8:00 pm	8:30 pm
9:00 pm	9:30 pm

DAY / DATE ______________________________

MY GOALS TODAY

____

____

____

____

____

____

NOTES

TIME BLOCKS

3:00 am	3:30 am
4:00 am	4:30 am
5:00 am	5:30 am
6:00 am	6:30 am
7:00 am	7:30 am
8:00 am	8:30 am
9:00 am	9:30 am
10:00 am	10:30 am
11:00 am	11:30 am
12:00 pm	12:30 pm
1:00 pm	1:30 pm
2:00 pm	2:30 pm
3:00 pm	3:30 pm
4:00 pm	4:30 pm
5:00 pm	5:30 pm
6:00 pm	6:30 pm
7:00 pm	7:30 pm
8:00 pm	8:30 pm
9:00 pm	9:30 pm

DAY / DATE ______________________

MY GOALS TODAY

____
____
____
____
____
____

NOTES

TIME BLOCKS

3:00 am	3:30 am
4:00 am	4:30 am
5:00 am	5:30 am
6:00 am	6:30 am
7:00 am	7:30 am
8:00 am	8:30 am
9:00 am	9:30 am
10:00 am	10:30 am
11:00 am	11:30 am
12:00 pm	12:30 pm
1:00 pm	1:30 pm
2:00 pm	2:30 pm
3:00 pm	3:30 pm
4:00 pm	4:30 pm
5:00 pm	5:30 pm
6:00 pm	6:30 pm
7:00 pm	7:30 pm
8:00 pm	8:30 pm
9:00 pm	9:30 pm

DAY / DATE ____________________

MY GOALS TODAY

____
____
____
____
____
____

NOTES

TIME BLOCKS

3:00 am	3:30 am
4:00 am	4:30 am
5:00 am	5:30 am
6:00 am	6:30 am
7:00 am	7:30 am
8:00 am	8:30 am
9:00 am	9:30 am
10:00 am	10:30 am
11:00 am	11:30 am
12:00 pm	12:30 pm
1:00 pm	1:30 pm
2:00 pm	2:30 pm
3:00 pm	3:30 pm
4:00 pm	4:30 pm
5:00 pm	5:30 pm
6:00 pm	6:30 pm
7:00 pm	7:30 pm
8:00 pm	8:30 pm
9:00 pm	9:30 pm

DAY / DATE ______________________________

MY GOALS TODAY

____

____

____

____

____

____

NOTES

TIME BLOCKS

3:00 am	3:30 am
4:00 am	4:30 am
5:00 am	5:30 am
6:00 am	6:30 am
7:00 am	7:30 am
8:00 am	8:30 am
9:00 am	9:30 am
10:00 am	10:30 am
11:00 am	11:30 am
12:00 pm	12:30 pm
1:00 pm	1:30 pm
2:00 pm	2:30 pm
3:00 pm	3:30 pm
4:00 pm	4:30 pm
5:00 pm	5:30 pm
6:00 pm	6:30 pm
7:00 pm	7:30 pm
8:00 pm	8:30 pm
9:00 pm	9:30 pm

Thoughts become words. Words become action. Actions become character. Character becomes destiny.

DAY / DATE ____________________

MY GOALS TODAY

____

____

____

____

____

____

NOTES

TIME BLOCKS

3:00 am	3:30 am
4:00 am	4:30 am
5:00 am	5:30 am
6:00 am	6:30 am
7:00 am	7:30 am
8:00 am	8:30 am
9:00 am	9:30 am
10:00 am	10:30 am
11:00 am	11:30 am
12:00 pm	12:30 pm
1:00 pm	1:30 pm
2:00 pm	2:30 pm
3:00 pm	3:30 pm
4:00 pm	4:30 pm
5:00 pm	5:30 pm
6:00 pm	6:30 pm
7:00 pm	7:30 pm
8:00 pm	8:30 pm
9:00 pm	9:30 pm

DAY / DATE ____________________

MY GOALS TODAY

____
____
____
____
____
____

NOTES

TIME BLOCKS

3:00 am	3:30 am
4:00 am	4:30 am
5:00 am	5:30 am
6:00 am	6:30 am
7:00 am	7:30 am
8:00 am	8:30 am
9:00 am	9:30 am
10:00 am	10:30 am
11:00 am	11:30 am
12:00 pm	12:30 pm
1:00 pm	1:30 pm
2:00 pm	2:30 pm
3:00 pm	3:30 pm
4:00 pm	4:30 pm
5:00 pm	5:30 pm
6:00 pm	6:30 pm
7:00 pm	7:30 pm
8:00 pm	8:30 pm
9:00 pm	9:30 pm

DAY / DATE ______________________________

MY GOALS TODAY

____
____
____
____
____
____

NOTES

TIME BLOCKS

3:00 am	3:30 am
4:00 am	4:30 am
5:00 am	5:30 am
6:00 am	6:30 am
7:00 am	7:30 am
8:00 am	8:30 am
9:00 am	9:30 am
10:00 am	10:30 am
11:00 am	11:30 am
12:00 pm	12:30 pm
1:00 pm	1:30 pm
2:00 pm	2:30 pm
3:00 pm	3:30 pm
4:00 pm	4:30 pm
5:00 pm	5:30 pm
6:00 pm	6:30 pm
7:00 pm	7:30 pm
8:00 pm	8:30 pm
9:00 pm	9:30 pm

DAY / DATE ______________________________

MY GOALS TODAY

____

____

____

____

____

____

TIME BLOCKS

3:00 am	3:30 am
4:00 am	4:30 am
5:00 am	5:30 am
6:00 am	6:30 am
7:00 am	7:30 am
8:00 am	8:30 am
9:00 am	9:30 am
10:00 am	10:30 am
11:00 am	11:30 am
12:00 pm	12:30 pm
1:00 pm	1:30 pm
2:00 pm	2:30 pm
3:00 pm	3:30 pm
4:00 pm	4:30 pm
5:00 pm	5:30 pm
6:00 pm	6:30 pm
7:00 pm	7:30 pm
8:00 pm	8:30 pm
9:00 pm	9:30 pm

NOTES

Thoughts become words. Words become action. Actions become character. Character becomes destiny.

DAY / DATE ____________________

MY GOALS TODAY

____

____

____

____

____

____

NOTES

TIME BLOCKS

3:00 am	3:30 am
4:00 am	4:30 am
5:00 am	5:30 am
6:00 am	6:30 am
7:00 am	7:30 am
8:00 am	8:30 am
9:00 am	9:30 am
10:00 am	10:30 am
11:00 am	11:30 am
12:00 pm	12:30 pm
1:00 pm	1:30 pm
2:00 pm	2:30 pm
3:00 pm	3:30 pm
4:00 pm	4:30 pm
5:00 pm	5:30 pm
6:00 pm	6:30 pm
7:00 pm	7:30 pm
8:00 pm	8:30 pm
9:00 pm	9:30 pm

DAY / DATE ______________________________

MY GOALS TODAY

____
____
____
____
____
____

NOTES

TIME BLOCKS

3:00 am	3:30 am
4:00 am	4:30 am
5:00 am	5:30 am
6:00 am	6:30 am
7:00 am	7:30 am
8:00 am	8:30 am
9:00 am	9:30 am
10:00 am	10:30 am
11:00 am	11:30 am
12:00 pm	12:30 pm
1:00 pm	1:30 pm
2:00 pm	2:30 pm
3:00 pm	3:30 pm
4:00 pm	4:30 pm
5:00 pm	5:30 pm
6:00 pm	6:30 pm
7:00 pm	7:30 pm
8:00 pm	8:30 pm
9:00 pm	9:30 pm

DAY / DATE ____________________

MY GOALS TODAY

____

____

____

____

____

____

NOTES

TIME BLOCKS

3:00 am	3:30 am
4:00 am	4:30 am
5:00 am	5:30 am
6:00 am	6:30 am
7:00 am	7:30 am
8:00 am	8:30 am
9:00 am	9:30 am
10:00 am	10:30 am
11:00 am	11:30 am
12:00 pm	12:30 pm
1:00 pm	1:30 pm
2:00 pm	2:30 pm
3:00 pm	3:30 pm
4:00 pm	4:30 pm
5:00 pm	5:30 pm
6:00 pm	6:30 pm
7:00 pm	7:30 pm
8:00 pm	8:30 pm
9:00 pm	9:30 pm

DAY / DATE ____

MY GOALS TODAY

____

____

____

____

____

____

NOTES

TIME BLOCKS

3:00 am	3:30 am
4:00 am	4:30 am
5:00 am	5:30 am
6:00 am	6:30 am
7:00 am	7:30 am
8:00 am	8:30 am
9:00 am	9:30 am
10:00 am	10:30 am
11:00 am	11:30 am
12:00 pm	12:30 pm
1:00 pm	1:30 pm
2:00 pm	2:30 pm
3:00 pm	3:30 pm
4:00 pm	4:30 pm
5:00 pm	5:30 pm
6:00 pm	6:30 pm
7:00 pm	7:30 pm
8:00 pm	8:30 pm
9:00 pm	9:30 pm

DAY / DATE ____________________

MY GOALS TODAY

NOTES

TIME BLOCKS

3:00 am	3:30 am
4:00 am	4:30 am
5:00 am	5:30 am
6:00 am	6:30 am
7:00 am	7:30 am
8:00 am	8:30 am
9:00 am	9:30 am
10:00 am	10:30 am
11:00 am	11:30 am
12:00 pm	12:30 pm
1:00 pm	1:30 pm
2:00 pm	2:30 pm
3:00 pm	3:30 pm
4:00 pm	4:30 pm
5:00 pm	5:30 pm
6:00 pm	6:30 pm
7:00 pm	7:30 pm
8:00 pm	8:30 pm
9:00 pm	9:30 pm

DAY / DATE ______________________________

MY GOALS TODAY

____
____
____
____
____
____

NOTES

TIME BLOCKS

3:00 am	3:30 am
4:00 am	4:30 am
5:00 am	5:30 am
6:00 am	6:30 am
7:00 am	7:30 am
8:00 am	8:30 am
9:00 am	9:30 am
10:00 am	10:30 am
11:00 am	11:30 am
12:00 pm	12:30 pm
1:00 pm	1:30 pm
2:00 pm	2:30 pm
3:00 pm	3:30 pm
4:00 pm	4:30 pm
5:00 pm	5:30 pm
6:00 pm	6:30 pm
7:00 pm	7:30 pm
8:00 pm	8:30 pm
9:00 pm	9:30 pm

DAY / DATE ______________________________

MY GOALS TODAY

____
____
____
____
____
____

NOTES

TIME BLOCKS

3:00 am	3:30 am
4:00 am	4:30 am
5:00 am	5:30 am
6:00 am	6:30 am
7:00 am	7:30 am
8:00 am	8:30 am
9:00 am	9:30 am
10:00 am	10:30 am
11:00 am	11:30 am
12:00 pm	12:30 pm
1:00 pm	1:30 pm
2:00 pm	2:30 pm
3:00 pm	3:30 pm
4:00 pm	4:30 pm
5:00 pm	5:30 pm
6:00 pm	6:30 pm
7:00 pm	7:30 pm
8:00 pm	8:30 pm
9:00 pm	9:30 pm

DAY / DATE ____________________

MY GOALS TODAY

____

____

____

____

____

____

NOTES

TIME BLOCKS

3:00 am	3:30 am
4:00 am	4:30 am
5:00 am	5:30 am
6:00 am	6:30 am
7:00 am	7:30 am
8:00 am	8:30 am
9:00 am	9:30 am
10:00 am	10:30 am
11:00 am	11:30 am
12:00 pm	12:30 pm
1:00 pm	1:30 pm
2:00 pm	2:30 pm
3:00 pm	3:30 pm
4:00 pm	4:30 pm
5:00 pm	5:30 pm
6:00 pm	6:30 pm
7:00 pm	7:30 pm
8:00 pm	8:30 pm
9:00 pm	9:30 pm

DAY / DATE ______________________________

MY GOALS TODAY

____

____

____

____

____

____

NOTES

TIME BLOCKS

3:00 am	3:30 am
4:00 am	4:30 am
5:00 am	5:30 am
6:00 am	6:30 am
7:00 am	7:30 am
8:00 am	8:30 am
9:00 am	9:30 am
10:00 am	10:30 am
11:00 am	11:30 am
12:00 pm	12:30 pm
1:00 pm	1:30 pm
2:00 pm	2:30 pm
3:00 pm	3:30 pm
4:00 pm	4:30 pm
5:00 pm	5:30 pm
6:00 pm	6:30 pm
7:00 pm	7:30 pm
8:00 pm	8:30 pm
9:00 pm	9:30 pm

DAY / DATE ______________________________

MY GOALS TODAY

____
____
____
____
____
____

NOTES

TIME BLOCKS

3:00 am	3:30 am
4:00 am	4:30 am
5:00 am	5:30 am
6:00 am	6:30 am
7:00 am	7:30 am
8:00 am	8:30 am
9:00 am	9:30 am
10:00 am	10:30 am
11:00 am	11:30 am
12:00 pm	12:30 pm
1:00 pm	1:30 pm
2:00 pm	2:30 pm
3:00 pm	3:30 pm
4:00 pm	4:30 pm
5:00 pm	5:30 pm
6:00 pm	6:30 pm
7:00 pm	7:30 pm
8:00 pm	8:30 pm
9:00 pm	9:30 pm

DAY / DATE ______________________________

MY GOALS TODAY

____

____

____

____

____

____

NOTES

TIME BLOCKS

3:00 am	3:30 am
4:00 am	4:30 am
5:00 am	5:30 am
6:00 am	6:30 am
7:00 am	7:30 am
8:00 am	8:30 am
9:00 am	9:30 am
10:00 am	10:30 am
11:00 am	11:30 am
12:00 pm	12:30 pm
1:00 pm	1:30 pm
2:00 pm	2:30 pm
3:00 pm	3:30 pm
4:00 pm	4:30 pm
5:00 pm	5:30 pm
6:00 pm	6:30 pm
7:00 pm	7:30 pm
8:00 pm	8:30 pm
9:00 pm	9:30 pm

DAY / DATE ____________________

MY GOALS TODAY

____

____

____

____

____

____

NOTES

TIME BLOCKS

3:00 am	3:30 am
4:00 am	4:30 am
5:00 am	5:30 am
6:00 am	6:30 am
7:00 am	7:30 am
8:00 am	8:30 am
9:00 am	9:30 am
10:00 am	10:30 am
11:00 am	11:30 am
12:00 pm	12:30 pm
1:00 pm	1:30 pm
2:00 pm	2:30 pm
3:00 pm	3:30 pm
4:00 pm	4:30 pm
5:00 pm	5:30 pm
6:00 pm	6:30 pm
7:00 pm	7:30 pm
8:00 pm	8:30 pm
9:00 pm	9:30 pm

DAY / DATE ____________________

MY GOALS TODAY

____

____

____

____

____

____

NOTES

TIME BLOCKS

3:00 am	3:30 am
4:00 am	4:30 am
5:00 am	5:30 am
6:00 am	6:30 am
7:00 am	7:30 am
8:00 am	8:30 am
9:00 am	9:30 am
10:00 am	10:30 am
11:00 am	11:30 am
12:00 pm	12:30 pm
1:00 pm	1:30 pm
2:00 pm	2:30 pm
3:00 pm	3:30 pm
4:00 pm	4:30 pm
5:00 pm	5:30 pm
6:00 pm	6:30 pm
7:00 pm	7:30 pm
8:00 pm	8:30 pm
9:00 pm	9:30 pm

DAY / DATE ______________________________

MY GOALS TODAY

____

____

____

____

____

____

NOTES

TIME BLOCKS

3:00 am	3:30 am
4:00 am	4:30 am
5:00 am	5:30 am
6:00 am	6:30 am
7:00 am	7:30 am
8:00 am	8:30 am
9:00 am	9:30 am
10:00 am	10:30 am
11:00 am	11:30 am
12:00 pm	12:30 pm
1:00 pm	1:30 pm
2:00 pm	2:30 pm
3:00 pm	3:30 pm
4:00 pm	4:30 pm
5:00 pm	5:30 pm
6:00 pm	6:30 pm
7:00 pm	7:30 pm
8:00 pm	8:30 pm
9:00 pm	9:30 pm

DAY / DATE ______________________________

MY GOALS TODAY

____

____

____

____

____

____

NOTES

TIME BLOCKS

3:00 am	3:30 am
4:00 am	4:30 am
5:00 am	5:30 am
6:00 am	6:30 am
7:00 am	7:30 am
8:00 am	8:30 am
9:00 am	9:30 am
10:00 am	10:30 am
11:00 am	11:30 am
12:00 pm	12:30 pm
1:00 pm	1:30 pm
2:00 pm	2:30 pm
3:00 pm	3:30 pm
4:00 pm	4:30 pm
5:00 pm	5:30 pm
6:00 pm	6:30 pm
7:00 pm	7:30 pm
8:00 pm	8:30 pm
9:00 pm	9:30 pm

DAY / DATE ______________________________

MY GOALS TODAY

____

____

____

____

____

____

NOTES

TIME BLOCKS

3:00 am	3:30 am
4:00 am	4:30 am
5:00 am	5:30 am
6:00 am	6:30 am
7:00 am	7:30 am
8:00 am	8:30 am
9:00 am	9:30 am
10:00 am	10:30 am
11:00 am	11:30 am
12:00 pm	12:30 pm
1:00 pm	1:30 pm
2:00 pm	2:30 pm
3:00 pm	3:30 pm
4:00 pm	4:30 pm
5:00 pm	5:30 pm
6:00 pm	6:30 pm
7:00 pm	7:30 pm
8:00 pm	8:30 pm
9:00 pm	9:30 pm

DAY / DATE ______________________________

MY GOALS TODAY

____
____
____
____
____
____

NOTES

TIME BLOCKS

3:00 am	3:30 am
4:00 am	4:30 am
5:00 am	5:30 am
6:00 am	6:30 am
7:00 am	7:30 am
8:00 am	8:30 am
9:00 am	9:30 am
10:00 am	10:30 am
11:00 am	11:30 am
12:00 pm	12:30 pm
1:00 pm	1:30 pm
2:00 pm	2:30 pm
3:00 pm	3:30 pm
4:00 pm	4:30 pm
5:00 pm	5:30 pm
6:00 pm	6:30 pm
7:00 pm	7:30 pm
8:00 pm	8:30 pm
9:00 pm	9:30 pm

DAY / DATE ______________________________

MY GOALS TODAY

____

____

____

____

____

____

NOTES

TIME BLOCKS

3:00 am	3:30 am
4:00 am	4:30 am
5:00 am	5:30 am
6:00 am	6:30 am
7:00 am	7:30 am
8:00 am	8:30 am
9:00 am	9:30 am
10:00 am	10:30 am
11:00 am	11:30 am
12:00 pm	12:30 pm
1:00 pm	1:30 pm
2:00 pm	2:30 pm
3:00 pm	3:30 pm
4:00 pm	4:30 pm
5:00 pm	5:30 pm
6:00 pm	6:30 pm
7:00 pm	7:30 pm
8:00 pm	8:30 pm
9:00 pm	9:30 pm

DAY / DATE ____________________

MY GOALS TODAY

____

____

____

____

____

____

NOTES

TIME BLOCKS

3:00 am	3:30 am
4:00 am	4:30 am
5:00 am	5:30 am
6:00 am	6:30 am
7:00 am	7:30 am
8:00 am	8:30 am
9:00 am	9:30 am
10:00 am	10:30 am
11:00 am	11:30 am
12:00 pm	12:30 pm
1:00 pm	1:30 pm
2:00 pm	2:30 pm
3:00 pm	3:30 pm
4:00 pm	4:30 pm
5:00 pm	5:30 pm
6:00 pm	6:30 pm
7:00 pm	7:30 pm
8:00 pm	8:30 pm
9:00 pm	9:30 pm

DAY / DATE ______________________________

MY GOALS TODAY

____

____

____

____

____

____

NOTES

TIME BLOCKS

3:00 am	3:30 am
4:00 am	4:30 am
5:00 am	5:30 am
6:00 am	6:30 am
7:00 am	7:30 am
8:00 am	8:30 am
9:00 am	9:30 am
10:00 am	10:30 am
11:00 am	11:30 am
12:00 pm	12:30 pm
1:00 pm	1:30 pm
2:00 pm	2:30 pm
3:00 pm	3:30 pm
4:00 pm	4:30 pm
5:00 pm	5:30 pm
6:00 pm	6:30 pm
7:00 pm	7:30 pm
8:00 pm	8:30 pm
9:00 pm	9:30 pm

DAY / DATE ______________________________

MY GOALS TODAY

____

____

____

____

____

____

NOTES

TIME BLOCKS

3:00 am	3:30 am
4:00 am	4:30 am
5:00 am	5:30 am
6:00 am	6:30 am
7:00 am	7:30 am
8:00 am	8:30 am
9:00 am	9:30 am
10:00 am	10:30 am
11:00 am	11:30 am
12:00 pm	12:30 pm
1:00 pm	1:30 pm
2:00 pm	2:30 pm
3:00 pm	3:30 pm
4:00 pm	4:30 pm
5:00 pm	5:30 pm
6:00 pm	6:30 pm
7:00 pm	7:30 pm
8:00 pm	8:30 pm
9:00 pm	9:30 pm

DAY / DATE ______________________________

MY GOALS TODAY

____
____
____
____
____
____

NOTES

TIME BLOCKS

3:00 am	3:30 am
4:00 am	4:30 am
5:00 am	5:30 am
6:00 am	6:30 am
7:00 am	7:30 am
8:00 am	8:30 am
9:00 am	9:30 am
10:00 am	10:30 am
11:00 am	11:30 am
12:00 pm	12:30 pm
1:00 pm	1:30 pm
2:00 pm	2:30 pm
3:00 pm	3:30 pm
4:00 pm	4:30 pm
5:00 pm	5:30 pm
6:00 pm	6:30 pm
7:00 pm	7:30 pm
8:00 pm	8:30 pm
9:00 pm	9:30 pm

DAY / DATE ______________________________

MY GOALS TODAY

____

____

____

____

____

____

NOTES

TIME BLOCKS

3:00 am	3:30 am
4:00 am	4:30 am
5:00 am	5:30 am
6:00 am	6:30 am
7:00 am	7:30 am
8:00 am	8:30 am
9:00 am	9:30 am
10:00 am	10:30 am
11:00 am	11:30 am
12:00 pm	12:30 pm
1:00 pm	1:30 pm
2:00 pm	2:30 pm
3:00 pm	3:30 pm
4:00 pm	4:30 pm
5:00 pm	5:30 pm
6:00 pm	6:30 pm
7:00 pm	7:30 pm
8:00 pm	8:30 pm
9:00 pm	9:30 pm

DAY / DATE ______________________

MY GOALS TODAY

____
____
____
____
____
____

NOTES

TIME BLOCKS

3:00 am	3:30 am
4:00 am	4:30 am
5:00 am	5:30 am
6:00 am	6:30 am
7:00 am	7:30 am
8:00 am	8:30 am
9:00 am	9:30 am
10:00 am	10:30 am
11:00 am	11:30 am
12:00 pm	12:30 pm
1:00 pm	1:30 pm
2:00 pm	2:30 pm
3:00 pm	3:30 pm
4:00 pm	4:30 pm
5:00 pm	5:30 pm
6:00 pm	6:30 pm
7:00 pm	7:30 pm
8:00 pm	8:30 pm
9:00 pm	9:30 pm

DAY / DATE ______________________________

MY GOALS TODAY

____

____

____

____

____

____

NOTES

TIME BLOCKS

3:00 am	3:30 am
4:00 am	4:30 am
5:00 am	5:30 am
6:00 am	6:30 am
7:00 am	7:30 am
8:00 am	8:30 am
9:00 am	9:30 am
10:00 am	10:30 am
11:00 am	11:30 am
12:00 pm	12:30 pm
1:00 pm	1:30 pm
2:00 pm	2:30 pm
3:00 pm	3:30 pm
4:00 pm	4:30 pm
5:00 pm	5:30 pm
6:00 pm	6:30 pm
7:00 pm	7:30 pm
8:00 pm	8:30 pm
9:00 pm	9:30 pm

DAY / DATE ____________________

MY GOALS TODAY

NOTES

TIME BLOCKS

3:00 am	3:30 am
4:00 am	4:30 am
5:00 am	5:30 am
6:00 am	6:30 am
7:00 am	7:30 am
8:00 am	8:30 am
9:00 am	9:30 am
10:00 am	10:30 am
11:00 am	11:30 am
12:00 pm	12:30 pm
1:00 pm	1:30 pm
2:00 pm	2:30 pm
3:00 pm	3:30 pm
4:00 pm	4:30 pm
5:00 pm	5:30 pm
6:00 pm	6:30 pm
7:00 pm	7:30 pm
8:00 pm	8:30 pm
9:00 pm	9:30 pm

DAY / DATE ______________________________

MY GOALS TODAY

____
____
____
____
____
____

NOTES

TIME BLOCKS

3:00 am	3:30 am
4:00 am	4:30 am
5:00 am	5:30 am
6:00 am	6:30 am
7:00 am	7:30 am
8:00 am	8:30 am
9:00 am	9:30 am
10:00 am	10:30 am
11:00 am	11:30 am
12:00 pm	12:30 pm
1:00 pm	1:30 pm
2:00 pm	2:30 pm
3:00 pm	3:30 pm
4:00 pm	4:30 pm
5:00 pm	5:30 pm
6:00 pm	6:30 pm
7:00 pm	7:30 pm
8:00 pm	8:30 pm
9:00 pm	9:30 pm

DAY / DATE ____________________

MY GOALS TODAY

____
____
____
____
____
____

NOTES

TIME BLOCKS

3:00 am	3:30 am
4:00 am	4:30 am
5:00 am	5:30 am
6:00 am	6:30 am
7:00 am	7:30 am
8:00 am	8:30 am
9:00 am	9:30 am
10:00 am	10:30 am
11:00 am	11:30 am
12:00 pm	12:30 pm
1:00 pm	1:30 pm
2:00 pm	2:30 pm
3:00 pm	3:30 pm
4:00 pm	4:30 pm
5:00 pm	5:30 pm
6:00 pm	6:30 pm
7:00 pm	7:30 pm
8:00 pm	8:30 pm
9:00 pm	9:30 pm

DAY / DATE ______________________________

MY GOALS TODAY

____

____

____

____

____

____

NOTES

TIME BLOCKS

3:00 am	3:30 am
4:00 am	4:30 am
5:00 am	5:30 am
6:00 am	6:30 am
7:00 am	7:30 am
8:00 am	8:30 am
9:00 am	9:30 am
10:00 am	10:30 am
11:00 am	11:30 am
12:00 pm	12:30 pm
1:00 pm	1:30 pm
2:00 pm	2:30 pm
3:00 pm	3:30 pm
4:00 pm	4:30 pm
5:00 pm	5:30 pm
6:00 pm	6:30 pm
7:00 pm	7:30 pm
8:00 pm	8:30 pm
9:00 pm	9:30 pm

DAY / DATE ______________________________

MY GOALS TODAY

____

____

____

____

____

____

NOTES

TIME BLOCKS

3:00 am	3:30 am
4:00 am	4:30 am
5:00 am	5:30 am
6:00 am	6:30 am
7:00 am	7:30 am
8:00 am	8:30 am
9:00 am	9:30 am
10:00 am	10:30 am
11:00 am	11:30 am
12:00 pm	12:30 pm
1:00 pm	1:30 pm
2:00 pm	2:30 pm
3:00 pm	3:30 pm
4:00 pm	4:30 pm
5:00 pm	5:30 pm
6:00 pm	6:30 pm
7:00 pm	7:30 pm
8:00 pm	8:30 pm
9:00 pm	9:30 pm

DAY / DATE ______________________________

MY GOALS TODAY

____

____

____

____

____

____

NOTES

TIME BLOCKS

3:00 am	3:30 am
4:00 am	4:30 am
5:00 am	5:30 am
6:00 am	6:30 am
7:00 am	7:30 am
8:00 am	8:30 am
9:00 am	9:30 am
10:00 am	10:30 am
11:00 am	11:30 am
12:00 pm	12:30 pm
1:00 pm	1:30 pm
2:00 pm	2:30 pm
3:00 pm	3:30 pm
4:00 pm	4:30 pm
5:00 pm	5:30 pm
6:00 pm	6:30 pm
7:00 pm	7:30 pm
8:00 pm	8:30 pm
9:00 pm	9:30 pm

DAY / DATE ____________________

MY GOALS TODAY

____

____

____

____

____

____

NOTES

TIME BLOCKS

3:00 am	3:30 am
4:00 am	4:30 am
5:00 am	5:30 am
6:00 am	6:30 am
7:00 am	7:30 am
8:00 am	8:30 am
9:00 am	9:30 am
10:00 am	10:30 am
11:00 am	11:30 am
12:00 pm	12:30 pm
1:00 pm	1:30 pm
2:00 pm	2:30 pm
3:00 pm	3:30 pm
4:00 pm	4:30 pm
5:00 pm	5:30 pm
6:00 pm	6:30 pm
7:00 pm	7:30 pm
8:00 pm	8:30 pm
9:00 pm	9:30 pm

DAY / DATE ____________________

MY GOALS TODAY

____
____
____
____
____
____

NOTES

TIME BLOCKS

3:00 am	3:30 am
4:00 am	4:30 am
5:00 am	5:30 am
6:00 am	6:30 am
7:00 am	7:30 am
8:00 am	8:30 am
9:00 am	9:30 am
10:00 am	10:30 am
11:00 am	11:30 am
12:00 pm	12:30 pm
1:00 pm	1:30 pm
2:00 pm	2:30 pm
3:00 pm	3:30 pm
4:00 pm	4:30 pm
5:00 pm	5:30 pm
6:00 pm	6:30 pm
7:00 pm	7:30 pm
8:00 pm	8:30 pm
9:00 pm	9:30 pm

DAY / DATE ______________________________

MY GOALS TODAY

____

____

____

____

____

____

NOTES

TIME BLOCKS

3:00 am	3:30 am
4:00 am	4:30 am
5:00 am	5:30 am
6:00 am	6:30 am
7:00 am	7:30 am
8:00 am	8:30 am
9:00 am	9:30 am
10:00 am	10:30 am
11:00 am	11:30 am
12:00 pm	12:30 pm
1:00 pm	1:30 pm
2:00 pm	2:30 pm
3:00 pm	3:30 pm
4:00 pm	4:30 pm
5:00 pm	5:30 pm
6:00 pm	6:30 pm
7:00 pm	7:30 pm
8:00 pm	8:30 pm
9:00 pm	9:30 pm

DAY / DATE ____________________

MY GOALS TODAY

____

____

____

____

____

____

NOTES

TIME BLOCKS

3:00 am	3:30 am
4:00 am	4:30 am
5:00 am	5:30 am
6:00 am	6:30 am
7:00 am	7:30 am
8:00 am	8:30 am
9:00 am	9:30 am
10:00 am	10:30 am
11:00 am	11:30 am
12:00 pm	12:30 pm
1:00 pm	1:30 pm
2:00 pm	2:30 pm
3:00 pm	3:30 pm
4:00 pm	4:30 pm
5:00 pm	5:30 pm
6:00 pm	6:30 pm
7:00 pm	7:30 pm
8:00 pm	8:30 pm
9:00 pm	9:30 pm

DAY / DATE ____________________

MY GOALS TODAY

____

____

____

____

____

____

NOTES

TIME BLOCKS

3:00 am	3:30 am
4:00 am	4:30 am
5:00 am	5:30 am
6:00 am	6:30 am
7:00 am	7:30 am
8:00 am	8:30 am
9:00 am	9:30 am
10:00 am	10:30 am
11:00 am	11:30 am
12:00 pm	12:30 pm
1:00 pm	1:30 pm
2:00 pm	2:30 pm
3:00 pm	3:30 pm
4:00 pm	4:30 pm
5:00 pm	5:30 pm
6:00 pm	6:30 pm
7:00 pm	7:30 pm
8:00 pm	8:30 pm
9:00 pm	9:30 pm

DAY / DATE ____________________

MY GOALS TODAY

____

____

____

____

____

____

NOTES

TIME BLOCKS

3:00 am	3:30 am
4:00 am	4:30 am
5:00 am	5:30 am
6:00 am	6:30 am
7:00 am	7:30 am
8:00 am	8:30 am
9:00 am	9:30 am
10:00 am	10:30 am
11:00 am	11:30 am
12:00 pm	12:30 pm
1:00 pm	1:30 pm
2:00 pm	2:30 pm
3:00 pm	3:30 pm
4:00 pm	4:30 pm
5:00 pm	5:30 pm
6:00 pm	6:30 pm
7:00 pm	7:30 pm
8:00 pm	8:30 pm
9:00 pm	9:30 pm

DAY / DATE ______________________________

MY GOALS TODAY

____

____

____

____

____

____

NOTES

TIME BLOCKS

3:00 am	3:30 am
4:00 am	4:30 am
5:00 am	5:30 am
6:00 am	6:30 am
7:00 am	7:30 am
8:00 am	8:30 am
9:00 am	9:30 am
10:00 am	10:30 am
11:00 am	11:30 am
12:00 pm	12:30 pm
1:00 pm	1:30 pm
2:00 pm	2:30 pm
3:00 pm	3:30 pm
4:00 pm	4:30 pm
5:00 pm	5:30 pm
6:00 pm	6:30 pm
7:00 pm	7:30 pm
8:00 pm	8:30 pm
9:00 pm	9:30 pm

DAY / DATE ______________________________

MY GOALS TODAY

____

____

____

____

____

____

NOTES

TIME BLOCKS

3:00 am	3:30 am
4:00 am	4:30 am
5:00 am	5:30 am
6:00 am	6:30 am
7:00 am	7:30 am
8:00 am	8:30 am
9:00 am	9:30 am
10:00 am	10:30 am
11:00 am	11:30 am
12:00 pm	12:30 pm
1:00 pm	1:30 pm
2:00 pm	2:30 pm
3:00 pm	3:30 pm
4:00 pm	4:30 pm
5:00 pm	5:30 pm
6:00 pm	6:30 pm
7:00 pm	7:30 pm
8:00 pm	8:30 pm
9:00 pm	9:30 pm

DAY / DATE ______________________________

MY GOALS TODAY

____
____
____
____
____
____

NOTES

TIME BLOCKS

3:00 am	3:30 am
4:00 am	4:30 am
5:00 am	5:30 am
6:00 am	6:30 am
7:00 am	7:30 am
8:00 am	8:30 am
9:00 am	9:30 am
10:00 am	10:30 am
11:00 am	11:30 am
12:00 pm	12:30 pm
1:00 pm	1:30 pm
2:00 pm	2:30 pm
3:00 pm	3:30 pm
4:00 pm	4:30 pm
5:00 pm	5:30 pm
6:00 pm	6:30 pm
7:00 pm	7:30 pm
8:00 pm	8:30 pm
9:00 pm	9:30 pm

Thoughts become words. Words become action. Actions become character. Character becomes destiny.

TIME MASTERY AND BLOCKER

DAY / DATE ______________________________

MY GOALS TODAY

____

____

____

____

____

____

NOTES

TIME BLOCKS

3:00 am	3:30 am
4:00 am	4:30 am
5:00 am	5:30 am
6:00 am	6:30 am
7:00 am	7:30 am
8:00 am	8:30 am
9:00 am	9:30 am
10:00 am	10:30 am
11:00 am	11:30 am
12:00 pm	12:30 pm
1:00 pm	1:30 pm
2:00 pm	2:30 pm
3:00 pm	3:30 pm
4:00 pm	4:30 pm
5:00 pm	5:30 pm
6:00 pm	6:30 pm
7:00 pm	7:30 pm
8:00 pm	8:30 pm
9:00 pm	9:30 pm

DAY / DATE ______________________________

MY GOALS TODAY

____
____
____
____
____
____

NOTES

TIME BLOCKS

3:00 am	3:30 am
4:00 am	4:30 am
5:00 am	5:30 am
6:00 am	6:30 am
7:00 am	7:30 am
8:00 am	8:30 am
9:00 am	9:30 am
10:00 am	10:30 am
11:00 am	11:30 am
12:00 pm	12:30 pm
1:00 pm	1:30 pm
2:00 pm	2:30 pm
3:00 pm	3:30 pm
4:00 pm	4:30 pm
5:00 pm	5:30 pm
6:00 pm	6:30 pm
7:00 pm	7:30 pm
8:00 pm	8:30 pm
9:00 pm	9:30 pm

DAY / DATE ______________________________

MY GOALS TODAY

____

____

____

____

____

____

NOTES

TIME BLOCKS

3:00 am	3:30 am
4:00 am	4:30 am
5:00 am	5:30 am
6:00 am	6:30 am
7:00 am	7:30 am
8:00 am	8:30 am
9:00 am	9:30 am
10:00 am	10:30 am
11:00 am	11:30 am
12:00 pm	12:30 pm
1:00 pm	1:30 pm
2:00 pm	2:30 pm
3:00 pm	3:30 pm
4:00 pm	4:30 pm
5:00 pm	5:30 pm
6:00 pm	6:30 pm
7:00 pm	7:30 pm
8:00 pm	8:30 pm
9:00 pm	9:30 pm

DAY / DATE ____________________

MY GOALS TODAY

____
____
____
____
____
____

NOTES

TIME BLOCKS

3:00 am	3:30 am
4:00 am	4:30 am
5:00 am	5:30 am
6:00 am	6:30 am
7:00 am	7:30 am
8:00 am	8:30 am
9:00 am	9:30 am
10:00 am	10:30 am
11:00 am	11:30 am
12:00 pm	12:30 pm
1:00 pm	1:30 pm
2:00 pm	2:30 pm
3:00 pm	3:30 pm
4:00 pm	4:30 pm
5:00 pm	5:30 pm
6:00 pm	6:30 pm
7:00 pm	7:30 pm
8:00 pm	8:30 pm
9:00 pm	9:30 pm

DAY / DATE ______________________________

MY GOALS TODAY

____
____
____
____
____
____

NOTES

TIME BLOCKS

3:00 am	3:30 am
4:00 am	4:30 am
5:00 am	5:30 am
6:00 am	6:30 am
7:00 am	7:30 am
8:00 am	8:30 am
9:00 am	9:30 am
10:00 am	10:30 am
11:00 am	11:30 am
12:00 pm	12:30 pm
1:00 pm	1:30 pm
2:00 pm	2:30 pm
3:00 pm	3:30 pm
4:00 pm	4:30 pm
5:00 pm	5:30 pm
6:00 pm	6:30 pm
7:00 pm	7:30 pm
8:00 pm	8:30 pm
9:00 pm	9:30 pm

DAY / DATE ______________________________

MY GOALS TODAY

____
____
____
____
____
____

NOTES

TIME BLOCKS

3:00 am	3:30 am
4:00 am	4:30 am
5:00 am	5:30 am
6:00 am	6:30 am
7:00 am	7:30 am
8:00 am	8:30 am
9:00 am	9:30 am
10:00 am	10:30 am
11:00 am	11:30 am
12:00 pm	12:30 pm
1:00 pm	1:30 pm
2:00 pm	2:30 pm
3:00 pm	3:30 pm
4:00 pm	4:30 pm
5:00 pm	5:30 pm
6:00 pm	6:30 pm
7:00 pm	7:30 pm
8:00 pm	8:30 pm
9:00 pm	9:30 pm

DAY / DATE ______________________________

MY GOALS TODAY

____
____
____
____
____
____

NOTES

TIME BLOCKS

3:00 am	3:30 am
4:00 am	4:30 am
5:00 am	5:30 am
6:00 am	6:30 am
7:00 am	7:30 am
8:00 am	8:30 am
9:00 am	9:30 am
10:00 am	10:30 am
11:00 am	11:30 am
12:00 pm	12:30 pm
1:00 pm	1:30 pm
2:00 pm	2:30 pm
3:00 pm	3:30 pm
4:00 pm	4:30 pm
5:00 pm	5:30 pm
6:00 pm	6:30 pm
7:00 pm	7:30 pm
8:00 pm	8:30 pm
9:00 pm	9:30 pm

Thoughts become words. Words become action. Actions become character. Character becomes destiny.

DAY / DATE ______________________

MY GOALS TODAY

____
____
____
____
____
____

NOTES

TIME BLOCKS

3:00 am	3:30 am
4:00 am	4:30 am
5:00 am	5:30 am
6:00 am	6:30 am
7:00 am	7:30 am
8:00 am	8:30 am
9:00 am	9:30 am
10:00 am	10:30 am
11:00 am	11:30 am
12:00 pm	12:30 pm
1:00 pm	1:30 pm
2:00 pm	2:30 pm
3:00 pm	3:30 pm
4:00 pm	4:30 pm
5:00 pm	5:30 pm
6:00 pm	6:30 pm
7:00 pm	7:30 pm
8:00 pm	8:30 pm
9:00 pm	9:30 pm

DAY / DATE ______________________________

MY GOALS TODAY

____

____

____

____

____

____

NOTES

TIME BLOCKS

3:00 am	3:30 am
4:00 am	4:30 am
5:00 am	5:30 am
6:00 am	6:30 am
7:00 am	7:30 am
8:00 am	8:30 am
9:00 am	9:30 am
10:00 am	10:30 am
11:00 am	11:30 am
12:00 pm	12:30 pm
1:00 pm	1:30 pm
2:00 pm	2:30 pm
3:00 pm	3:30 pm
4:00 pm	4:30 pm
5:00 pm	5:30 pm
6:00 pm	6:30 pm
7:00 pm	7:30 pm
8:00 pm	8:30 pm
9:00 pm	9:30 pm

DAY / DATE ______________________________

MY GOALS TODAY

____
____
____
____
____
____

NOTES

TIME BLOCKS

3:00 am	3:30 am
4:00 am	4:30 am
5:00 am	5:30 am
6:00 am	6:30 am
7:00 am	7:30 am
8:00 am	8:30 am
9:00 am	9:30 am
10:00 am	10:30 am
11:00 am	11:30 am
12:00 pm	12:30 pm
1:00 pm	1:30 pm
2:00 pm	2:30 pm
3:00 pm	3:30 pm
4:00 pm	4:30 pm
5:00 pm	5:30 pm
6:00 pm	6:30 pm
7:00 pm	7:30 pm
8:00 pm	8:30 pm
9:00 pm	9:30 pm

DAY / DATE ______________________________

MY GOALS TODAY

____

____

____

____

____

____

NOTES

TIME BLOCKS

3:00 am	3:30 am
4:00 am	4:30 am
5:00 am	5:30 am
6:00 am	6:30 am
7:00 am	7:30 am
8:00 am	8:30 am
9:00 am	9:30 am
10:00 am	10:30 am
11:00 am	11:30 am
12:00 pm	12:30 pm
1:00 pm	1:30 pm
2:00 pm	2:30 pm
3:00 pm	3:30 pm
4:00 pm	4:30 pm
5:00 pm	5:30 pm
6:00 pm	6:30 pm
7:00 pm	7:30 pm
8:00 pm	8:30 pm
9:00 pm	9:30 pm

DAY / DATE ______________________

MY GOALS TODAY

____

____

____

____

____

____

NOTES

TIME BLOCKS

3:00 am	3:30 am
4:00 am	4:30 am
5:00 am	5:30 am
6:00 am	6:30 am
7:00 am	7:30 am
8:00 am	8:30 am
9:00 am	9:30 am
10:00 am	10:30 am
11:00 am	11:30 am
12:00 pm	12:30 pm
1:00 pm	1:30 pm
2:00 pm	2:30 pm
3:00 pm	3:30 pm
4:00 pm	4:30 pm
5:00 pm	5:30 pm
6:00 pm	6:30 pm
7:00 pm	7:30 pm
8:00 pm	8:30 pm
9:00 pm	9:30 pm

Thoughts become words. Words become action. Actions become character. Character becomes destiny.

TIME MASTERY AND BLOCKER

DAY / DATE ______________________________

MY GOALS TODAY

____

____

____

____

____

____

NOTES

TIME BLOCKS

3:00 am	3:30 am
4:00 am	4:30 am
5:00 am	5:30 am
6:00 am	6:30 am
7:00 am	7:30 am
8:00 am	8:30 am
9:00 am	9:30 am
10:00 am	10:30 am
11:00 am	11:30 am
12:00 pm	12:30 pm
1:00 pm	1:30 pm
2:00 pm	2:30 pm
3:00 pm	3:30 pm
4:00 pm	4:30 pm
5:00 pm	5:30 pm
6:00 pm	6:30 pm
7:00 pm	7:30 pm
8:00 pm	8:30 pm
9:00 pm	9:30 pm

DAY / DATE ______________________________

MY GOALS TODAY

____
____
____
____
____
____

NOTES

TIME BLOCKS

3:00 am	3:30 am
4:00 am	4:30 am
5:00 am	5:30 am
6:00 am	6:30 am
7:00 am	7:30 am
8:00 am	8:30 am
9:00 am	9:30 am
10:00 am	10:30 am
11:00 am	11:30 am
12:00 pm	12:30 pm
1:00 pm	1:30 pm
2:00 pm	2:30 pm
3:00 pm	3:30 pm
4:00 pm	4:30 pm
5:00 pm	5:30 pm
6:00 pm	6:30 pm
7:00 pm	7:30 pm
8:00 pm	8:30 pm
9:00 pm	9:30 pm

DAY / DATE ____________________

MY GOALS TODAY

____
____
____
____
____
____

NOTES

TIME BLOCKS

3:00 am	3:30 am
4:00 am	4:30 am
5:00 am	5:30 am
6:00 am	6:30 am
7:00 am	7:30 am
8:00 am	8:30 am
9:00 am	9:30 am
10:00 am	10:30 am
11:00 am	11:30 am
12:00 pm	12:30 pm
1:00 pm	1:30 pm
2:00 pm	2:30 pm
3:00 pm	3:30 pm
4:00 pm	4:30 pm
5:00 pm	5:30 pm
6:00 pm	6:30 pm
7:00 pm	7:30 pm
8:00 pm	8:30 pm
9:00 pm	9:30 pm

DAY / DATE ____________________

MY GOALS TODAY

______

______

______

______

______

______

NOTES

TIME BLOCKS

3:00 am	3:30 am
4:00 am	4:30 am
5:00 am	5:30 am
6:00 am	6:30 am
7:00 am	7:30 am
8:00 am	8:30 am
9:00 am	9:30 am
10:00 am	10:30 am
11:00 am	11:30 am
12:00 pm	12:30 pm
1:00 pm	1:30 pm
2:00 pm	2:30 pm
3:00 pm	3:30 pm
4:00 pm	4:30 pm
5:00 pm	5:30 pm
6:00 pm	6:30 pm
7:00 pm	7:30 pm
8:00 pm	8:30 pm
9:00 pm	9:30 pm

DAY / DATE ____________________

MY GOALS TODAY

____
____
____
____
____
____

NOTES

TIME BLOCKS

3:00 am	3:30 am
4:00 am	4:30 am
5:00 am	5:30 am
6:00 am	6:30 am
7:00 am	7:30 am
8:00 am	8:30 am
9:00 am	9:30 am
10:00 am	10:30 am
11:00 am	11:30 am
12:00 pm	12:30 pm
1:00 pm	1:30 pm
2:00 pm	2:30 pm
3:00 pm	3:30 pm
4:00 pm	4:30 pm
5:00 pm	5:30 pm
6:00 pm	6:30 pm
7:00 pm	7:30 pm
8:00 pm	8:30 pm
9:00 pm	9:30 pm

DAY / DATE ______________________________

MY GOALS TODAY

____
____
____
____
____
____

NOTES

TIME BLOCKS

3:00 am	3:30 am
4:00 am	4:30 am
5:00 am	5:30 am
6:00 am	6:30 am
7:00 am	7:30 am
8:00 am	8:30 am
9:00 am	9:30 am
10:00 am	10:30 am
11:00 am	11:30 am
12:00 pm	12:30 pm
1:00 pm	1:30 pm
2:00 pm	2:30 pm
3:00 pm	3:30 pm
4:00 pm	4:30 pm
5:00 pm	5:30 pm
6:00 pm	6:30 pm
7:00 pm	7:30 pm
8:00 pm	8:30 pm
9:00 pm	9:30 pm

DAY / DATE ______________________________

MY GOALS TODAY

____

____

____

____

____

____

NOTES

TIME BLOCKS

3:00 am	3:30 am
4:00 am	4:30 am
5:00 am	5:30 am
6:00 am	6:30 am
7:00 am	7:30 am
8:00 am	8:30 am
9:00 am	9:30 am
10:00 am	10:30 am
11:00 am	11:30 am
12:00 pm	12:30 pm
1:00 pm	1:30 pm
2:00 pm	2:30 pm
3:00 pm	3:30 pm
4:00 pm	4:30 pm
5:00 pm	5:30 pm
6:00 pm	6:30 pm
7:00 pm	7:30 pm
8:00 pm	8:30 pm
9:00 pm	9:30 pm

DAY / DATE ______________________________

MY GOALS TODAY

____
____
____
____
____
____

NOTES

TIME BLOCKS

3:00 am	3:30 am
4:00 am	4:30 am
5:00 am	5:30 am
6:00 am	6:30 am
7:00 am	7:30 am
8:00 am	8:30 am
9:00 am	9:30 am
10:00 am	10:30 am
11:00 am	11:30 am
12:00 pm	12:30 pm
1:00 pm	1:30 pm
2:00 pm	2:30 pm
3:00 pm	3:30 pm
4:00 pm	4:30 pm
5:00 pm	5:30 pm
6:00 pm	6:30 pm
7:00 pm	7:30 pm
8:00 pm	8:30 pm
9:00 pm	9:30 pm

DAY / DATE ______________________________

MY GOALS TODAY

____

____

____

____

____

____

NOTES

TIME BLOCKS

3:00 am	3:30 am
4:00 am	4:30 am
5:00 am	5:30 am
6:00 am	6:30 am
7:00 am	7:30 am
8:00 am	8:30 am
9:00 am	9:30 am
10:00 am	10:30 am
11:00 am	11:30 am
12:00 pm	12:30 pm
1:00 pm	1:30 pm
2:00 pm	2:30 pm
3:00 pm	3:30 pm
4:00 pm	4:30 pm
5:00 pm	5:30 pm
6:00 pm	6:30 pm
7:00 pm	7:30 pm
8:00 pm	8:30 pm
9:00 pm	9:30 pm

DAY / DATE ______________________________

MY GOALS TODAY

____
____
____
____
____
____

NOTES

TIME BLOCKS

3:00 am	3:30 am
4:00 am	4:30 am
5:00 am	5:30 am
6:00 am	6:30 am
7:00 am	7:30 am
8:00 am	8:30 am
9:00 am	9:30 am
10:00 am	10:30 am
11:00 am	11:30 am
12:00 pm	12:30 pm
1:00 pm	1:30 pm
2:00 pm	2:30 pm
3:00 pm	3:30 pm
4:00 pm	4:30 pm
5:00 pm	5:30 pm
6:00 pm	6:30 pm
7:00 pm	7:30 pm
8:00 pm	8:30 pm
9:00 pm	9:30 pm

DAY / DATE ______________________________

MY GOALS TODAY

____
____
____
____
____
____

NOTES

TIME BLOCKS

3:00 am	3:30 am
4:00 am	4:30 am
5:00 am	5:30 am
6:00 am	6:30 am
7:00 am	7:30 am
8:00 am	8:30 am
9:00 am	9:30 am
10:00 am	10:30 am
11:00 am	11:30 am
12:00 pm	12:30 pm
1:00 pm	1:30 pm
2:00 pm	2:30 pm
3:00 pm	3:30 pm
4:00 pm	4:30 pm
5:00 pm	5:30 pm
6:00 pm	6:30 pm
7:00 pm	7:30 pm
8:00 pm	8:30 pm
9:00 pm	9:30 pm

DAY / DATE ______________________________

MY GOALS TODAY

____
____
____
____
____
____

NOTES

TIME BLOCKS

3:00 am	3:30 am
4:00 am	4:30 am
5:00 am	5:30 am
6:00 am	6:30 am
7:00 am	7:30 am
8:00 am	8:30 am
9:00 am	9:30 am
10:00 am	10:30 am
11:00 am	11:30 am
12:00 pm	12:30 pm
1:00 pm	1:30 pm
2:00 pm	2:30 pm
3:00 pm	3:30 pm
4:00 pm	4:30 pm
5:00 pm	5:30 pm
6:00 pm	6:30 pm
7:00 pm	7:30 pm
8:00 pm	8:30 pm
9:00 pm	9:30 pm

DAY / DATE ______________________________

MY GOALS TODAY

____

____

____

____

____

____

NOTES

TIME BLOCKS

3:00 am	3:30 am
4:00 am	4:30 am
5:00 am	5:30 am
6:00 am	6:30 am
7:00 am	7:30 am
8:00 am	8:30 am
9:00 am	9:30 am
10:00 am	10:30 am
11:00 am	11:30 am
12:00 pm	12:30 pm
1:00 pm	1:30 pm
2:00 pm	2:30 pm
3:00 pm	3:30 pm
4:00 pm	4:30 pm
5:00 pm	5:30 pm
6:00 pm	6:30 pm
7:00 pm	7:30 pm
8:00 pm	8:30 pm
9:00 pm	9:30 pm

DAY / DATE ______________________________

MY GOALS TODAY

____

____

____

____

____

____

NOTES

TIME BLOCKS

3:00 am	3:30 am
4:00 am	4:30 am
5:00 am	5:30 am
6:00 am	6:30 am
7:00 am	7:30 am
8:00 am	8:30 am
9:00 am	9:30 am
10:00 am	10:30 am
11:00 am	11:30 am
12:00 pm	12:30 pm
1:00 pm	1:30 pm
2:00 pm	2:30 pm
3:00 pm	3:30 pm
4:00 pm	4:30 pm
5:00 pm	5:30 pm
6:00 pm	6:30 pm
7:00 pm	7:30 pm
8:00 pm	8:30 pm
9:00 pm	9:30 pm

DAY / DATE ______________________________

MY GOALS TODAY

____

____

____

____

____

____

NOTES

TIME BLOCKS

3:00 am	3:30 am
4:00 am	4:30 am
5:00 am	5:30 am
6:00 am	6:30 am
7:00 am	7:30 am
8:00 am	8:30 am
9:00 am	9:30 am
10:00 am	10:30 am
11:00 am	11:30 am
12:00 pm	12:30 pm
1:00 pm	1:30 pm
2:00 pm	2:30 pm
3:00 pm	3:30 pm
4:00 pm	4:30 pm
5:00 pm	5:30 pm
6:00 pm	6:30 pm
7:00 pm	7:30 pm
8:00 pm	8:30 pm
9:00 pm	9:30 pm

DAY / DATE ______________________________

MY GOALS TODAY

____

____

____

____

____

____

NOTES

TIME BLOCKS

3:00 am	3:30 am
4:00 am	4:30 am
5:00 am	5:30 am
6:00 am	6:30 am
7:00 am	7:30 am
8:00 am	8:30 am
9:00 am	9:30 am
10:00 am	10:30 am
11:00 am	11:30 am
12:00 pm	12:30 pm
1:00 pm	1:30 pm
2:00 pm	2:30 pm
3:00 pm	3:30 pm
4:00 pm	4:30 pm
5:00 pm	5:30 pm
6:00 pm	6:30 pm
7:00 pm	7:30 pm
8:00 pm	8:30 pm
9:00 pm	9:30 pm

DAY / DATE ______________________________

MY GOALS TODAY

____

____

____

____

____

____

NOTES

TIME BLOCKS

3:00 am	3:30 am
4:00 am	4:30 am
5:00 am	5:30 am
6:00 am	6:30 am
7:00 am	7:30 am
8:00 am	8:30 am
9:00 am	9:30 am
10:00 am	10:30 am
11:00 am	11:30 am
12:00 pm	12:30 pm
1:00 pm	1:30 pm
2:00 pm	2:30 pm
3:00 pm	3:30 pm
4:00 pm	4:30 pm
5:00 pm	5:30 pm
6:00 pm	6:30 pm
7:00 pm	7:30 pm
8:00 pm	8:30 pm
9:00 pm	9:30 pm

DAY / DATE ____________________

MY GOALS TODAY

____

____

____

____

____

____

NOTES

TIME BLOCKS

3:00 am	3:30 am
4:00 am	4:30 am
5:00 am	5:30 am
6:00 am	6:30 am
7:00 am	7:30 am
8:00 am	8:30 am
9:00 am	9:30 am
10:00 am	10:30 am
11:00 am	11:30 am
12:00 pm	12:30 pm
1:00 pm	1:30 pm
2:00 pm	2:30 pm
3:00 pm	3:30 pm
4:00 pm	4:30 pm
5:00 pm	5:30 pm
6:00 pm	6:30 pm
7:00 pm	7:30 pm
8:00 pm	8:30 pm
9:00 pm	9:30 pm

DAY / DATE ______________________________

MY GOALS TODAY

____

____

____

____

____

____

NOTES

TIME BLOCKS

3:00 am	3:30 am
4:00 am	4:30 am
5:00 am	5:30 am
6:00 am	6:30 am
7:00 am	7:30 am
8:00 am	8:30 am
9:00 am	9:30 am
10:00 am	10:30 am
11:00 am	11:30 am
12:00 pm	12:30 pm
1:00 pm	1:30 pm
2:00 pm	2:30 pm
3:00 pm	3:30 pm
4:00 pm	4:30 pm
5:00 pm	5:30 pm
6:00 pm	6:30 pm
7:00 pm	7:30 pm
8:00 pm	8:30 pm
9:00 pm	9:30 pm

DAY / DATE ____________________

MY GOALS TODAY

____

____

____

____

____

____

NOTES

TIME BLOCKS

3:00 am	3:30 am
4:00 am	4:30 am
5:00 am	5:30 am
6:00 am	6:30 am
7:00 am	7:30 am
8:00 am	8:30 am
9:00 am	9:30 am
10:00 am	10:30 am
11:00 am	11:30 am
12:00 pm	12:30 pm
1:00 pm	1:30 pm
2:00 pm	2:30 pm
3:00 pm	3:30 pm
4:00 pm	4:30 pm
5:00 pm	5:30 pm
6:00 pm	6:30 pm
7:00 pm	7:30 pm
8:00 pm	8:30 pm
9:00 pm	9:30 pm

DAY / DATE ______________________________

MY GOALS TODAY

____

____

____

____

____

____

NOTES

TIME BLOCKS

3:00 am	3:30 am
4:00 am	4:30 am
5:00 am	5:30 am
6:00 am	6:30 am
7:00 am	7:30 am
8:00 am	8:30 am
9:00 am	9:30 am
10:00 am	10:30 am
11:00 am	11:30 am
12:00 pm	12:30 pm
1:00 pm	1:30 pm
2:00 pm	2:30 pm
3:00 pm	3:30 pm
4:00 pm	4:30 pm
5:00 pm	5:30 pm
6:00 pm	6:30 pm
7:00 pm	7:30 pm
8:00 pm	8:30 pm
9:00 pm	9:30 pm

DAY / DATE ______________________________

MY GOALS TODAY

____
____
____
____
____
____

NOTES

TIME BLOCKS

3:00 am	3:30 am
4:00 am	4:30 am
5:00 am	5:30 am
6:00 am	6:30 am
7:00 am	7:30 am
8:00 am	8:30 am
9:00 am	9:30 am
10:00 am	10:30 am
11:00 am	11:30 am
12:00 pm	12:30 pm
1:00 pm	1:30 pm
2:00 pm	2:30 pm
3:00 pm	3:30 pm
4:00 pm	4:30 pm
5:00 pm	5:30 pm
6:00 pm	6:30 pm
7:00 pm	7:30 pm
8:00 pm	8:30 pm
9:00 pm	9:30 pm

DAY / DATE ______________________________

MY GOALS TODAY

____

____

____

____

____

____

NOTES

TIME BLOCKS

3:00 am	3:30 am
4:00 am	4:30 am
5:00 am	5:30 am
6:00 am	6:30 am
7:00 am	7:30 am
8:00 am	8:30 am
9:00 am	9:30 am
10:00 am	10:30 am
11:00 am	11:30 am
12:00 pm	12:30 pm
1:00 pm	1:30 pm
2:00 pm	2:30 pm
3:00 pm	3:30 pm
4:00 pm	4:30 pm
5:00 pm	5:30 pm
6:00 pm	6:30 pm
7:00 pm	7:30 pm
8:00 pm	8:30 pm
9:00 pm	9:30 pm

DAY / DATE ______________________________

MY GOALS TODAY

____
____
____
____
____
____

NOTES

TIME BLOCKS

3:00 am	3:30 am
4:00 am	4:30 am
5:00 am	5:30 am
6:00 am	6:30 am
7:00 am	7:30 am
8:00 am	8:30 am
9:00 am	9:30 am
10:00 am	10:30 am
11:00 am	11:30 am
12:00 pm	12:30 pm
1:00 pm	1:30 pm
2:00 pm	2:30 pm
3:00 pm	3:30 pm
4:00 pm	4:30 pm
5:00 pm	5:30 pm
6:00 pm	6:30 pm
7:00 pm	7:30 pm
8:00 pm	8:30 pm
9:00 pm	9:30 pm

DAY / DATE ____________________

MY GOALS TODAY

____
____
____
____
____
____

NOTES

TIME BLOCKS

3:00 am	3:30 am
4:00 am	4:30 am
5:00 am	5:30 am
6:00 am	6:30 am
7:00 am	7:30 am
8:00 am	8:30 am
9:00 am	9:30 am
10:00 am	10:30 am
11:00 am	11:30 am
12:00 pm	12:30 pm
1:00 pm	1:30 pm
2:00 pm	2:30 pm
3:00 pm	3:30 pm
4:00 pm	4:30 pm
5:00 pm	5:30 pm
6:00 pm	6:30 pm
7:00 pm	7:30 pm
8:00 pm	8:30 pm
9:00 pm	9:30 pm

DAY / DATE ______________________________

MY GOALS TODAY

____

____

____

____

____

____

NOTES

TIME BLOCKS

3:00 am	3:30 am
4:00 am	4:30 am
5:00 am	5:30 am
6:00 am	6:30 am
7:00 am	7:30 am
8:00 am	8:30 am
9:00 am	9:30 am
10:00 am	10:30 am
11:00 am	11:30 am
12:00 pm	12:30 pm
1:00 pm	1:30 pm
2:00 pm	2:30 pm
3:00 pm	3:30 pm
4:00 pm	4:30 pm
5:00 pm	5:30 pm
6:00 pm	6:30 pm
7:00 pm	7:30 pm
8:00 pm	8:30 pm
9:00 pm	9:30 pm

DAY / DATE ______________________

MY GOALS TODAY

____

____

____

____

____

____

NOTES

TIME BLOCKS

3:00 am	3:30 am
4:00 am	4:30 am
5:00 am	5:30 am
6:00 am	6:30 am
7:00 am	7:30 am
8:00 am	8:30 am
9:00 am	9:30 am
10:00 am	10:30 am
11:00 am	11:30 am
12:00 pm	12:30 pm
1:00 pm	1:30 pm
2:00 pm	2:30 pm
3:00 pm	3:30 pm
4:00 pm	4:30 pm
5:00 pm	5:30 pm
6:00 pm	6:30 pm
7:00 pm	7:30 pm
8:00 pm	8:30 pm
9:00 pm	9:30 pm

DAY / DATE ______________________________

MY GOALS TODAY

____

____

____

____

____

____

NOTES

TIME BLOCKS

3:00 am	3:30 am
4:00 am	4:30 am
5:00 am	5:30 am
6:00 am	6:30 am
7:00 am	7:30 am
8:00 am	8:30 am
9:00 am	9:30 am
10:00 am	10:30 am
11:00 am	11:30 am
12:00 pm	12:30 pm
1:00 pm	1:30 pm
2:00 pm	2:30 pm
3:00 pm	3:30 pm
4:00 pm	4:30 pm
5:00 pm	5:30 pm
6:00 pm	6:30 pm
7:00 pm	7:30 pm
8:00 pm	8:30 pm
9:00 pm	9:30 pm

DAY / DATE ______________________________

MY GOALS TODAY

____
____
____
____
____
____

NOTES

TIME BLOCKS

3:00 am	3:30 am
4:00 am	4:30 am
5:00 am	5:30 am
6:00 am	6:30 am
7:00 am	7:30 am
8:00 am	8:30 am
9:00 am	9:30 am
10:00 am	10:30 am
11:00 am	11:30 am
12:00 pm	12:30 pm
1:00 pm	1:30 pm
2:00 pm	2:30 pm
3:00 pm	3:30 pm
4:00 pm	4:30 pm
5:00 pm	5:30 pm
6:00 pm	6:30 pm
7:00 pm	7:30 pm
8:00 pm	8:30 pm
9:00 pm	9:30 pm

DAY / DATE ____________________

MY GOALS TODAY

____
____
____
____
____
____

NOTES

TIME BLOCKS

3:00 am	3:30 am
4:00 am	4:30 am
5:00 am	5:30 am
6:00 am	6:30 am
7:00 am	7:30 am
8:00 am	8:30 am
9:00 am	9:30 am
10:00 am	10:30 am
11:00 am	11:30 am
12:00 pm	12:30 pm
1:00 pm	1:30 pm
2:00 pm	2:30 pm
3:00 pm	3:30 pm
4:00 pm	4:30 pm
5:00 pm	5:30 pm
6:00 pm	6:30 pm
7:00 pm	7:30 pm
8:00 pm	8:30 pm
9:00 pm	9:30 pm

DAY / DATE ______________________________

MY GOALS TODAY

____
____
____
____
____
____

NOTES

TIME BLOCKS

3:00 am	3:30 am
4:00 am	4:30 am
5:00 am	5:30 am
6:00 am	6:30 am
7:00 am	7:30 am
8:00 am	8:30 am
9:00 am	9:30 am
10:00 am	10:30 am
11:00 am	11:30 am
12:00 pm	12:30 pm
1:00 pm	1:30 pm
2:00 pm	2:30 pm
3:00 pm	3:30 pm
4:00 pm	4:30 pm
5:00 pm	5:30 pm
6:00 pm	6:30 pm
7:00 pm	7:30 pm
8:00 pm	8:30 pm
9:00 pm	9:30 pm

DAY / DATE ____________________

MY GOALS TODAY

____
____
____
____
____
____

NOTES

TIME BLOCKS

3:00 am	3:30 am
4:00 am	4:30 am
5:00 am	5:30 am
6:00 am	6:30 am
7:00 am	7:30 am
8:00 am	8:30 am
9:00 am	9:30 am
10:00 am	10:30 am
11:00 am	11:30 am
12:00 pm	12:30 pm
1:00 pm	1:30 pm
2:00 pm	2:30 pm
3:00 pm	3:30 pm
4:00 pm	4:30 pm
5:00 pm	5:30 pm
6:00 pm	6:30 pm
7:00 pm	7:30 pm
8:00 pm	8:30 pm
9:00 pm	9:30 pm

TIME MASTERY AND BLOCKER

DAY / DATE ______________________________

MY GOALS TODAY

____

____

____

____

____

____

NOTES

TIME BLOCKS

3:00 am	3:30 am
4:00 am	4:30 am
5:00 am	5:30 am
6:00 am	6:30 am
7:00 am	7:30 am
8:00 am	8:30 am
9:00 am	9:30 am
10:00 am	10:30 am
11:00 am	11:30 am
12:00 pm	12:30 pm
1:00 pm	1:30 pm
2:00 pm	2:30 pm
3:00 pm	3:30 pm
4:00 pm	4:30 pm
5:00 pm	5:30 pm
6:00 pm	6:30 pm
7:00 pm	7:30 pm
8:00 pm	8:30 pm
9:00 pm	9:30 pm

DAY / DATE ____________________

MY GOALS TODAY

____
____
____
____
____
____

NOTES

TIME BLOCKS

3:00 am	3:30 am
4:00 am	4:30 am
5:00 am	5:30 am
6:00 am	6:30 am
7:00 am	7:30 am
8:00 am	8:30 am
9:00 am	9:30 am
10:00 am	10:30 am
11:00 am	11:30 am
12:00 pm	12:30 pm
1:00 pm	1:30 pm
2:00 pm	2:30 pm
3:00 pm	3:30 pm
4:00 pm	4:30 pm
5:00 pm	5:30 pm
6:00 pm	6:30 pm
7:00 pm	7:30 pm
8:00 pm	8:30 pm
9:00 pm	9:30 pm

DAY / DATE ____________________

MY GOALS TODAY

____

____

____

____

____

____

NOTES

TIME BLOCKS

3:00 am	3:30 am
4:00 am	4:30 am
5:00 am	5:30 am
6:00 am	6:30 am
7:00 am	7:30 am
8:00 am	8:30 am
9:00 am	9:30 am
10:00 am	10:30 am
11:00 am	11:30 am
12:00 pm	12:30 pm
1:00 pm	1:30 pm
2:00 pm	2:30 pm
3:00 pm	3:30 pm
4:00 pm	4:30 pm
5:00 pm	5:30 pm
6:00 pm	6:30 pm
7:00 pm	7:30 pm
8:00 pm	8:30 pm
9:00 pm	9:30 pm

DAY / DATE ______________________________

MY GOALS TODAY

____

____

____

____

____

____

NOTES

TIME BLOCKS

3:00 am	3:30 am
4:00 am	4:30 am
5:00 am	5:30 am
6:00 am	6:30 am
7:00 am	7:30 am
8:00 am	8:30 am
9:00 am	9:30 am
10:00 am	10:30 am
11:00 am	11:30 am
12:00 pm	12:30 pm
1:00 pm	1:30 pm
2:00 pm	2:30 pm
3:00 pm	3:30 pm
4:00 pm	4:30 pm
5:00 pm	5:30 pm
6:00 pm	6:30 pm
7:00 pm	7:30 pm
8:00 pm	8:30 pm
9:00 pm	9:30 pm

DAY / DATE ____________________

MY GOALS TODAY

____

____

____

____

____

____

NOTES

TIME BLOCKS

3:00 am	3:30 am
4:00 am	4:30 am
5:00 am	5:30 am
6:00 am	6:30 am
7:00 am	7:30 am
8:00 am	8:30 am
9:00 am	9:30 am
10:00 am	10:30 am
11:00 am	11:30 am
12:00 pm	12:30 pm
1:00 pm	1:30 pm
2:00 pm	2:30 pm
3:00 pm	3:30 pm
4:00 pm	4:30 pm
5:00 pm	5:30 pm
6:00 pm	6:30 pm
7:00 pm	7:30 pm
8:00 pm	8:30 pm
9:00 pm	9:30 pm

DAY / DATE ______________________________

MY GOALS TODAY

____

____

____

____

____

____

NOTES

TIME BLOCKS

3:00 am	3:30 am
4:00 am	4:30 am
5:00 am	5:30 am
6:00 am	6:30 am
7:00 am	7:30 am
8:00 am	8:30 am
9:00 am	9:30 am
10:00 am	10:30 am
11:00 am	11:30 am
12:00 pm	12:30 pm
1:00 pm	1:30 pm
2:00 pm	2:30 pm
3:00 pm	3:30 pm
4:00 pm	4:30 pm
5:00 pm	5:30 pm
6:00 pm	6:30 pm
7:00 pm	7:30 pm
8:00 pm	8:30 pm
9:00 pm	9:30 pm

DAY / DATE ____________________

MY GOALS TODAY

____

____

____

____

____

____

NOTES

TIME BLOCKS

3:00 am	3:30 am
4:00 am	4:30 am
5:00 am	5:30 am
6:00 am	6:30 am
7:00 am	7:30 am
8:00 am	8:30 am
9:00 am	9:30 am
10:00 am	10:30 am
11:00 am	11:30 am
12:00 pm	12:30 pm
1:00 pm	1:30 pm
2:00 pm	2:30 pm
3:00 pm	3:30 pm
4:00 pm	4:30 pm
5:00 pm	5:30 pm
6:00 pm	6:30 pm
7:00 pm	7:30 pm
8:00 pm	8:30 pm
9:00 pm	9:30 pm

DAY / DATE ____________________

MY GOALS TODAY

____
____
____
____
____
____

NOTES

TIME BLOCKS

3:00 am	3:30 am
4:00 am	4:30 am
5:00 am	5:30 am
6:00 am	6:30 am
7:00 am	7:30 am
8:00 am	8:30 am
9:00 am	9:30 am
10:00 am	10:30 am
11:00 am	11:30 am
12:00 pm	12:30 pm
1:00 pm	1:30 pm
2:00 pm	2:30 pm
3:00 pm	3:30 pm
4:00 pm	4:30 pm
5:00 pm	5:30 pm
6:00 pm	6:30 pm
7:00 pm	7:30 pm
8:00 pm	8:30 pm
9:00 pm	9:30 pm

DAY / DATE ___________________________

MY GOALS TODAY

____

____

____

____

____

____

NOTES

TIME BLOCKS

3:00 am	3:30 am
4:00 am	4:30 am
5:00 am	5:30 am
6:00 am	6:30 am
7:00 am	7:30 am
8:00 am	8:30 am
9:00 am	9:30 am
10:00 am	10:30 am
11:00 am	11:30 am
12:00 pm	12:30 pm
1:00 pm	1:30 pm
2:00 pm	2:30 pm
3:00 pm	3:30 pm
4:00 pm	4:30 pm
5:00 pm	5:30 pm
6:00 pm	6:30 pm
7:00 pm	7:30 pm
8:00 pm	8:30 pm
9:00 pm	9:30 pm

DAY / DATE ______________________________

MY GOALS TODAY

____
____
____
____
____
____

NOTES

TIME BLOCKS

3:00 am	3:30 am
4:00 am	4:30 am
5:00 am	5:30 am
6:00 am	6:30 am
7:00 am	7:30 am
8:00 am	8:30 am
9:00 am	9:30 am
10:00 am	10:30 am
11:00 am	11:30 am
12:00 pm	12:30 pm
1:00 pm	1:30 pm
2:00 pm	2:30 pm
3:00 pm	3:30 pm
4:00 pm	4:30 pm
5:00 pm	5:30 pm
6:00 pm	6:30 pm
7:00 pm	7:30 pm
8:00 pm	8:30 pm
9:00 pm	9:30 pm

DAY / DATE ____________________

MY GOALS TODAY

____

____

____

____

____

____

NOTES

TIME BLOCKS

3:00 am	3:30 am
4:00 am	4:30 am
5:00 am	5:30 am
6:00 am	6:30 am
7:00 am	7:30 am
8:00 am	8:30 am
9:00 am	9:30 am
10:00 am	10:30 am
11:00 am	11:30 am
12:00 pm	12:30 pm
1:00 pm	1:30 pm
2:00 pm	2:30 pm
3:00 pm	3:30 pm
4:00 pm	4:30 pm
5:00 pm	5:30 pm
6:00 pm	6:30 pm
7:00 pm	7:30 pm
8:00 pm	8:30 pm
9:00 pm	9:30 pm

DAY / DATE ______________________________

MY GOALS TODAY

____
____
____
____
____
____

NOTES

TIME BLOCKS

3:00 am	3:30 am
4:00 am	4:30 am
5:00 am	5:30 am
6:00 am	6:30 am
7:00 am	7:30 am
8:00 am	8:30 am
9:00 am	9:30 am
10:00 am	10:30 am
11:00 am	11:30 am
12:00 pm	12:30 pm
1:00 pm	1:30 pm
2:00 pm	2:30 pm
3:00 pm	3:30 pm
4:00 pm	4:30 pm
5:00 pm	5:30 pm
6:00 pm	6:30 pm
7:00 pm	7:30 pm
8:00 pm	8:30 pm
9:00 pm	9:30 pm

DAY / DATE ____________________

MY GOALS TODAY

____

____

____

____

____

____

NOTES

TIME BLOCKS

3:00 am	3:30 am
4:00 am	4:30 am
5:00 am	5:30 am
6:00 am	6:30 am
7:00 am	7:30 am
8:00 am	8:30 am
9:00 am	9:30 am
10:00 am	10:30 am
11:00 am	11:30 am
12:00 pm	12:30 pm
1:00 pm	1:30 pm
2:00 pm	2:30 pm
3:00 pm	3:30 pm
4:00 pm	4:30 pm
5:00 pm	5:30 pm
6:00 pm	6:30 pm
7:00 pm	7:30 pm
8:00 pm	8:30 pm
9:00 pm	9:30 pm

DAY / DATE ______________________________

MY GOALS TODAY

____
____
____
____
____
____

NOTES

TIME BLOCKS

3:00 am	3:30 am
4:00 am	4:30 am
5:00 am	5:30 am
6:00 am	6:30 am
7:00 am	7:30 am
8:00 am	8:30 am
9:00 am	9:30 am
10:00 am	10:30 am
11:00 am	11:30 am
12:00 pm	12:30 pm
1:00 pm	1:30 pm
2:00 pm	2:30 pm
3:00 pm	3:30 pm
4:00 pm	4:30 pm
5:00 pm	5:30 pm
6:00 pm	6:30 pm
7:00 pm	7:30 pm
8:00 pm	8:30 pm
9:00 pm	9:30 pm

DAY / DATE ______________________________

MY GOALS TODAY

____

____

____

____

____

____

NOTES

TIME BLOCKS

3:00 am	3:30 am
4:00 am	4:30 am
5:00 am	5:30 am
6:00 am	6:30 am
7:00 am	7:30 am
8:00 am	8:30 am
9:00 am	9:30 am
10:00 am	10:30 am
11:00 am	11:30 am
12:00 pm	12:30 pm
1:00 pm	1:30 pm
2:00 pm	2:30 pm
3:00 pm	3:30 pm
4:00 pm	4:30 pm
5:00 pm	5:30 pm
6:00 pm	6:30 pm
7:00 pm	7:30 pm
8:00 pm	8:30 pm
9:00 pm	9:30 pm

DAY / DATE ______________________________

MY GOALS TODAY

____
____
____
____
____
____

NOTES

TIME BLOCKS

3:00 am	3:30 am
4:00 am	4:30 am
5:00 am	5:30 am
6:00 am	6:30 am
7:00 am	7:30 am
8:00 am	8:30 am
9:00 am	9:30 am
10:00 am	10:30 am
11:00 am	11:30 am
12:00 pm	12:30 pm
1:00 pm	1:30 pm
2:00 pm	2:30 pm
3:00 pm	3:30 pm
4:00 pm	4:30 pm
5:00 pm	5:30 pm
6:00 pm	6:30 pm
7:00 pm	7:30 pm
8:00 pm	8:30 pm
9:00 pm	9:30 pm

DAY / DATE ____________________

MY GOALS TODAY

____

____

____

____

____

____

NOTES

TIME BLOCKS

3:00 am	3:30 am
4:00 am	4:30 am
5:00 am	5:30 am
6:00 am	6:30 am
7:00 am	7:30 am
8:00 am	8:30 am
9:00 am	9:30 am
10:00 am	10:30 am
11:00 am	11:30 am
12:00 pm	12:30 pm
1:00 pm	1:30 pm
2:00 pm	2:30 pm
3:00 pm	3:30 pm
4:00 pm	4:30 pm
5:00 pm	5:30 pm
6:00 pm	6:30 pm
7:00 pm	7:30 pm
8:00 pm	8:30 pm
9:00 pm	9:30 pm

DAY / DATE ______________________________

MY GOALS TODAY

____
____
____
____
____
____

NOTES

TIME BLOCKS

3:00 am	3:30 am
4:00 am	4:30 am
5:00 am	5:30 am
6:00 am	6:30 am
7:00 am	7:30 am
8:00 am	8:30 am
9:00 am	9:30 am
10:00 am	10:30 am
11:00 am	11:30 am
12:00 pm	12:30 pm
1:00 pm	1:30 pm
2:00 pm	2:30 pm
3:00 pm	3:30 pm
4:00 pm	4:30 pm
5:00 pm	5:30 pm
6:00 pm	6:30 pm
7:00 pm	7:30 pm
8:00 pm	8:30 pm
9:00 pm	9:30 pm

DAY / DATE ______________________________

MY GOALS TODAY

____

____

____

____

____

____

NOTES

TIME BLOCKS

3:00 am	3:30 am
4:00 am	4:30 am
5:00 am	5:30 am
6:00 am	6:30 am
7:00 am	7:30 am
8:00 am	8:30 am
9:00 am	9:30 am
10:00 am	10:30 am
11:00 am	11:30 am
12:00 pm	12:30 pm
1:00 pm	1:30 pm
2:00 pm	2:30 pm
3:00 pm	3:30 pm
4:00 pm	4:30 pm
5:00 pm	5:30 pm
6:00 pm	6:30 pm
7:00 pm	7:30 pm
8:00 pm	8:30 pm
9:00 pm	9:30 pm

DAY / DATE ______________________________

MY GOALS TODAY

____

____

____

____

____

____

NOTES

TIME BLOCKS

3:00 am	3:30 am
4:00 am	4:30 am
5:00 am	5:30 am
6:00 am	6:30 am
7:00 am	7:30 am
8:00 am	8:30 am
9:00 am	9:30 am
10:00 am	10:30 am
11:00 am	11:30 am
12:00 pm	12:30 pm
1:00 pm	1:30 pm
2:00 pm	2:30 pm
3:00 pm	3:30 pm
4:00 pm	4:30 pm
5:00 pm	5:30 pm
6:00 pm	6:30 pm
7:00 pm	7:30 pm
8:00 pm	8:30 pm
9:00 pm	9:30 pm

DAY / DATE ______________________________

MY GOALS TODAY

____

____

____

____

____

____

NOTES

TIME BLOCKS

3:00 am	3:30 am
4:00 am	4:30 am
5:00 am	5:30 am
6:00 am	6:30 am
7:00 am	7:30 am
8:00 am	8:30 am
9:00 am	9:30 am
10:00 am	10:30 am
11:00 am	11:30 am
12:00 pm	12:30 pm
1:00 pm	1:30 pm
2:00 pm	2:30 pm
3:00 pm	3:30 pm
4:00 pm	4:30 pm
5:00 pm	5:30 pm
6:00 pm	6:30 pm
7:00 pm	7:30 pm
8:00 pm	8:30 pm
9:00 pm	9:30 pm

DAY / DATE ____________________

MY GOALS TODAY

____

____

____

____

____

____

NOTES

TIME BLOCKS

3:00 am	3:30 am
4:00 am	4:30 am
5:00 am	5:30 am
6:00 am	6:30 am
7:00 am	7:30 am
8:00 am	8:30 am
9:00 am	9:30 am
10:00 am	10:30 am
11:00 am	11:30 am
12:00 pm	12:30 pm
1:00 pm	1:30 pm
2:00 pm	2:30 pm
3:00 pm	3:30 pm
4:00 pm	4:30 pm
5:00 pm	5:30 pm
6:00 pm	6:30 pm
7:00 pm	7:30 pm
8:00 pm	8:30 pm
9:00 pm	9:30 pm

DAY / DATE ______________________________

MY GOALS TODAY

____

____

____

____

____

____

NOTES

TIME BLOCKS

3:00 am	3:30 am
4:00 am	4:30 am
5:00 am	5:30 am
6:00 am	6:30 am
7:00 am	7:30 am
8:00 am	8:30 am
9:00 am	9:30 am
10:00 am	10:30 am
11:00 am	11:30 am
12:00 pm	12:30 pm
1:00 pm	1:30 pm
2:00 pm	2:30 pm
3:00 pm	3:30 pm
4:00 pm	4:30 pm
5:00 pm	5:30 pm
6:00 pm	6:30 pm
7:00 pm	7:30 pm
8:00 pm	8:30 pm
9:00 pm	9:30 pm

DAY / DATE ______________________________

MY GOALS TODAY

____
____
____
____
____
____

NOTES

TIME BLOCKS

3:00 am	3:30 am
4:00 am	4:30 am
5:00 am	5:30 am
6:00 am	6:30 am
7:00 am	7:30 am
8:00 am	8:30 am
9:00 am	9:30 am
10:00 am	10:30 am
11:00 am	11:30 am
12:00 pm	12:30 pm
1:00 pm	1:30 pm
2:00 pm	2:30 pm
3:00 pm	3:30 pm
4:00 pm	4:30 pm
5:00 pm	5:30 pm
6:00 pm	6:30 pm
7:00 pm	7:30 pm
8:00 pm	8:30 pm
9:00 pm	9:30 pm

DAY / DATE ______________________________

MY GOALS TODAY

____

____

____

____

____

____

NOTES

TIME BLOCKS

3:00 am	3:30 am
4:00 am	4:30 am
5:00 am	5:30 am
6:00 am	6:30 am
7:00 am	7:30 am
8:00 am	8:30 am
9:00 am	9:30 am
10:00 am	10:30 am
11:00 am	11:30 am
12:00 pm	12:30 pm
1:00 pm	1:30 pm
2:00 pm	2:30 pm
3:00 pm	3:30 pm
4:00 pm	4:30 pm
5:00 pm	5:30 pm
6:00 pm	6:30 pm
7:00 pm	7:30 pm
8:00 pm	8:30 pm
9:00 pm	9:30 pm

DAY / DATE ______________________________

MY GOALS TODAY

____

____

____

____

____

____

NOTES

TIME BLOCKS

3:00 am	3:30 am
4:00 am	4:30 am
5:00 am	5:30 am
6:00 am	6:30 am
7:00 am	7:30 am
8:00 am	8:30 am
9:00 am	9:30 am
10:00 am	10:30 am
11:00 am	11:30 am
12:00 pm	12:30 pm
1:00 pm	1:30 pm
2:00 pm	2:30 pm
3:00 pm	3:30 pm
4:00 pm	4:30 pm
5:00 pm	5:30 pm
6:00 pm	6:30 pm
7:00 pm	7:30 pm
8:00 pm	8:30 pm
9:00 pm	9:30 pm

DAY / DATE ______________________________

MY GOALS TODAY

____

____

____

____

____

____

NOTES

TIME BLOCKS

3:00 am	3:30 am
4:00 am	4:30 am
5:00 am	5:30 am
6:00 am	6:30 am
7:00 am	7:30 am
8:00 am	8:30 am
9:00 am	9:30 am
10:00 am	10:30 am
11:00 am	11:30 am
12:00 pm	12:30 pm
1:00 pm	1:30 pm
2:00 pm	2:30 pm
3:00 pm	3:30 pm
4:00 pm	4:30 pm
5:00 pm	5:30 pm
6:00 pm	6:30 pm
7:00 pm	7:30 pm
8:00 pm	8:30 pm
9:00 pm	9:30 pm

DAY / DATE ______________________________

MY GOALS TODAY

____

____

____

____

____

____

NOTES

TIME BLOCKS

3:00 am	3:30 am
4:00 am	4:30 am
5:00 am	5:30 am
6:00 am	6:30 am
7:00 am	7:30 am
8:00 am	8:30 am
9:00 am	9:30 am
10:00 am	10:30 am
11:00 am	11:30 am
12:00 pm	12:30 pm
1:00 pm	1:30 pm
2:00 pm	2:30 pm
3:00 pm	3:30 pm
4:00 pm	4:30 pm
5:00 pm	5:30 pm
6:00 pm	6:30 pm
7:00 pm	7:30 pm
8:00 pm	8:30 pm
9:00 pm	9:30 pm

DAY / DATE ______________________________

MY GOALS TODAY

____
____
____
____
____
____

NOTES

TIME BLOCKS

3:00 am	3:30 am
4:00 am	4:30 am
5:00 am	5:30 am
6:00 am	6:30 am
7:00 am	7:30 am
8:00 am	8:30 am
9:00 am	9:30 am
10:00 am	10:30 am
11:00 am	11:30 am
12:00 pm	12:30 pm
1:00 pm	1:30 pm
2:00 pm	2:30 pm
3:00 pm	3:30 pm
4:00 pm	4:30 pm
5:00 pm	5:30 pm
6:00 pm	6:30 pm
7:00 pm	7:30 pm
8:00 pm	8:30 pm
9:00 pm	9:30 pm

DAY / DATE ______________________________

MY GOALS TODAY

____
____
____
____
____
____

NOTES

TIME BLOCKS

3:00 am	3:30 am
4:00 am	4:30 am
5:00 am	5:30 am
6:00 am	6:30 am
7:00 am	7:30 am
8:00 am	8:30 am
9:00 am	9:30 am
10:00 am	10:30 am
11:00 am	11:30 am
12:00 pm	12:30 pm
1:00 pm	1:30 pm
2:00 pm	2:30 pm
3:00 pm	3:30 pm
4:00 pm	4:30 pm
5:00 pm	5:30 pm
6:00 pm	6:30 pm
7:00 pm	7:30 pm
8:00 pm	8:30 pm
9:00 pm	9:30 pm

DAY / DATE ____________________

MY GOALS TODAY

____

____

____

____

____

____

NOTES

TIME BLOCKS

3:00 am	3:30 am
4:00 am	4:30 am
5:00 am	5:30 am
6:00 am	6:30 am
7:00 am	7:30 am
8:00 am	8:30 am
9:00 am	9:30 am
10:00 am	10:30 am
11:00 am	11:30 am
12:00 pm	12:30 pm
1:00 pm	1:30 pm
2:00 pm	2:30 pm
3:00 pm	3:30 pm
4:00 pm	4:30 pm
5:00 pm	5:30 pm
6:00 pm	6:30 pm
7:00 pm	7:30 pm
8:00 pm	8:30 pm
9:00 pm	9:30 pm

DAY / DATE ______________________________

MY GOALS TODAY

____

____

____

____

____

____

NOTES

TIME BLOCKS

3:00 am	3:30 am
4:00 am	4:30 am
5:00 am	5:30 am
6:00 am	6:30 am
7:00 am	7:30 am
8:00 am	8:30 am
9:00 am	9:30 am
10:00 am	10:30 am
11:00 am	11:30 am
12:00 pm	12:30 pm
1:00 pm	1:30 pm
2:00 pm	2:30 pm
3:00 pm	3:30 pm
4:00 pm	4:30 pm
5:00 pm	5:30 pm
6:00 pm	6:30 pm
7:00 pm	7:30 pm
8:00 pm	8:30 pm
9:00 pm	9:30 pm

DAY / DATE ______________________________

MY GOALS TODAY

____

____

____

____

____

____

NOTES

TIME BLOCKS

3:00 am	3:30 am
4:00 am	4:30 am
5:00 am	5:30 am
6:00 am	6:30 am
7:00 am	7:30 am
8:00 am	8:30 am
9:00 am	9:30 am
10:00 am	10:30 am
11:00 am	11:30 am
12:00 pm	12:30 pm
1:00 pm	1:30 pm
2:00 pm	2:30 pm
3:00 pm	3:30 pm
4:00 pm	4:30 pm
5:00 pm	5:30 pm
6:00 pm	6:30 pm
7:00 pm	7:30 pm
8:00 pm	8:30 pm
9:00 pm	9:30 pm

TIME MASTERY AND BLOCKER

DAY / DATE ______________________________

MY GOALS TODAY

____

____

____

____

____

____

NOTES

TIME BLOCKS

3:00 am	3:30 am
4:00 am	4:30 am
5:00 am	5:30 am
6:00 am	6:30 am
7:00 am	7:30 am
8:00 am	8:30 am
9:00 am	9:30 am
10:00 am	10:30 am
11:00 am	11:30 am
12:00 pm	12:30 pm
1:00 pm	1:30 pm
2:00 pm	2:30 pm
3:00 pm	3:30 pm
4:00 pm	4:30 pm
5:00 pm	5:30 pm
6:00 pm	6:30 pm
7:00 pm	7:30 pm
8:00 pm	8:30 pm
9:00 pm	9:30 pm

DAY / DATE ______________________

MY GOALS TODAY

____

____

____

____

____

____

NOTES

TIME BLOCKS

3:00 am	3:30 am
4:00 am	4:30 am
5:00 am	5:30 am
6:00 am	6:30 am
7:00 am	7:30 am
8:00 am	8:30 am
9:00 am	9:30 am
10:00 am	10:30 am
11:00 am	11:30 am
12:00 pm	12:30 pm
1:00 pm	1:30 pm
2:00 pm	2:30 pm
3:00 pm	3:30 pm
4:00 pm	4:30 pm
5:00 pm	5:30 pm
6:00 pm	6:30 pm
7:00 pm	7:30 pm
8:00 pm	8:30 pm
9:00 pm	9:30 pm

DAY / DATE ______________________________

MY GOALS TODAY

____
____
____
____
____
____

NOTES

TIME BLOCKS

3:00 am	3:30 am
4:00 am	4:30 am
5:00 am	5:30 am
6:00 am	6:30 am
7:00 am	7:30 am
8:00 am	8:30 am
9:00 am	9:30 am
10:00 am	10:30 am
11:00 am	11:30 am
12:00 pm	12:30 pm
1:00 pm	1:30 pm
2:00 pm	2:30 pm
3:00 pm	3:30 pm
4:00 pm	4:30 pm
5:00 pm	5:30 pm
6:00 pm	6:30 pm
7:00 pm	7:30 pm
8:00 pm	8:30 pm
9:00 pm	9:30 pm

DAY / DATE ______________________________

MY GOALS TODAY

____
____
____
____
____
____

NOTES

TIME BLOCKS

3:00 am	3:30 am
4:00 am	4:30 am
5:00 am	5:30 am
6:00 am	6:30 am
7:00 am	7:30 am
8:00 am	8:30 am
9:00 am	9:30 am
10:00 am	10:30 am
11:00 am	11:30 am
12:00 pm	12:30 pm
1:00 pm	1:30 pm
2:00 pm	2:30 pm
3:00 pm	3:30 pm
4:00 pm	4:30 pm
5:00 pm	5:30 pm
6:00 pm	6:30 pm
7:00 pm	7:30 pm
8:00 pm	8:30 pm
9:00 pm	9:30 pm

DAY / DATE ______________________________

MY GOALS TODAY

____
____
____
____
____
____

NOTES

TIME BLOCKS

3:00 am	3:30 am
4:00 am	4:30 am
5:00 am	5:30 am
6:00 am	6:30 am
7:00 am	7:30 am
8:00 am	8:30 am
9:00 am	9:30 am
10:00 am	10:30 am
11:00 am	11:30 am
12:00 pm	12:30 pm
1:00 pm	1:30 pm
2:00 pm	2:30 pm
3:00 pm	3:30 pm
4:00 pm	4:30 pm
5:00 pm	5:30 pm
6:00 pm	6:30 pm
7:00 pm	7:30 pm
8:00 pm	8:30 pm
9:00 pm	9:30 pm

DAY / DATE ______________________________

MY GOALS TODAY

____

____

____

____

____

____

NOTES

TIME BLOCKS

3:00 am	3:30 am
4:00 am	4:30 am
5:00 am	5:30 am
6:00 am	6:30 am
7:00 am	7:30 am
8:00 am	8:30 am
9:00 am	9:30 am
10:00 am	10:30 am
11:00 am	11:30 am
12:00 pm	12:30 pm
1:00 pm	1:30 pm
2:00 pm	2:30 pm
3:00 pm	3:30 pm
4:00 pm	4:30 pm
5:00 pm	5:30 pm
6:00 pm	6:30 pm
7:00 pm	7:30 pm
8:00 pm	8:30 pm
9:00 pm	9:30 pm

DAY / DATE ______________________________

MY GOALS TODAY

____

____

____

____

____

____

NOTES

TIME BLOCKS

3:00 am	3:30 am
4:00 am	4:30 am
5:00 am	5:30 am
6:00 am	6:30 am
7:00 am	7:30 am
8:00 am	8:30 am
9:00 am	9:30 am
10:00 am	10:30 am
11:00 am	11:30 am
12:00 pm	12:30 pm
1:00 pm	1:30 pm
2:00 pm	2:30 pm
3:00 pm	3:30 pm
4:00 pm	4:30 pm
5:00 pm	5:30 pm
6:00 pm	6:30 pm
7:00 pm	7:30 pm
8:00 pm	8:30 pm
9:00 pm	9:30 pm

DAY / DATE ______________________________

MY GOALS TODAY

____

____

____

____

____

____

NOTES

TIME BLOCKS

3:00 am	3:30 am
4:00 am	4:30 am
5:00 am	5:30 am
6:00 am	6:30 am
7:00 am	7:30 am
8:00 am	8:30 am
9:00 am	9:30 am
10:00 am	10:30 am
11:00 am	11:30 am
12:00 pm	12:30 pm
1:00 pm	1:30 pm
2:00 pm	2:30 pm
3:00 pm	3:30 pm
4:00 pm	4:30 pm
5:00 pm	5:30 pm
6:00 pm	6:30 pm
7:00 pm	7:30 pm
8:00 pm	8:30 pm
9:00 pm	9:30 pm

DAY / DATE ______________________________

MY GOALS TODAY

____

____

____

____

____

____

NOTES

TIME BLOCKS

3:00 am	3:30 am
4:00 am	4:30 am
5:00 am	5:30 am
6:00 am	6:30 am
7:00 am	7:30 am
8:00 am	8:30 am
9:00 am	9:30 am
10:00 am	10:30 am
11:00 am	11:30 am
12:00 pm	12:30 pm
1:00 pm	1:30 pm
2:00 pm	2:30 pm
3:00 pm	3:30 pm
4:00 pm	4:30 pm
5:00 pm	5:30 pm
6:00 pm	6:30 pm
7:00 pm	7:30 pm
8:00 pm	8:30 pm
9:00 pm	9:30 pm

DAY / DATE ______________________________

MY GOALS TODAY

____
____
____
____
____
____

NOTES

TIME BLOCKS

3:00 am	3:30 am
4:00 am	4:30 am
5:00 am	5:30 am
6:00 am	6:30 am
7:00 am	7:30 am
8:00 am	8:30 am
9:00 am	9:30 am
10:00 am	10:30 am
11:00 am	11:30 am
12:00 pm	12:30 pm
1:00 pm	1:30 pm
2:00 pm	2:30 pm
3:00 pm	3:30 pm
4:00 pm	4:30 pm
5:00 pm	5:30 pm
6:00 pm	6:30 pm
7:00 pm	7:30 pm
8:00 pm	8:30 pm
9:00 pm	9:30 pm

DAY / DATE ______________________________

MY GOALS TODAY

____

____

____

____

____

____

NOTES

TIME BLOCKS

3:00 am	3:30 am
4:00 am	4:30 am
5:00 am	5:30 am
6:00 am	6:30 am
7:00 am	7:30 am
8:00 am	8:30 am
9:00 am	9:30 am
10:00 am	10:30 am
11:00 am	11:30 am
12:00 pm	12:30 pm
1:00 pm	1:30 pm
2:00 pm	2:30 pm
3:00 pm	3:30 pm
4:00 pm	4:30 pm
5:00 pm	5:30 pm
6:00 pm	6:30 pm
7:00 pm	7:30 pm
8:00 pm	8:30 pm
9:00 pm	9:30 pm

DAY / DATE ______________________________

MY GOALS TODAY

____

____

____

____

____

____

NOTES

TIME BLOCKS

3:00 am	3:30 am
4:00 am	4:30 am
5:00 am	5:30 am
6:00 am	6:30 am
7:00 am	7:30 am
8:00 am	8:30 am
9:00 am	9:30 am
10:00 am	10:30 am
11:00 am	11:30 am
12:00 pm	12:30 pm
1:00 pm	1:30 pm
2:00 pm	2:30 pm
3:00 pm	3:30 pm
4:00 pm	4:30 pm
5:00 pm	5:30 pm
6:00 pm	6:30 pm
7:00 pm	7:30 pm
8:00 pm	8:30 pm
9:00 pm	9:30 pm

Thoughts become words. Words become action. Actions become character. Character becomes destiny.

DAY / DATE ____________________

MY GOALS TODAY

____
____
____
____
____
____

NOTES

TIME BLOCKS

3:00 am	3:30 am
4:00 am	4:30 am
5:00 am	5:30 am
6:00 am	6:30 am
7:00 am	7:30 am
8:00 am	8:30 am
9:00 am	9:30 am
10:00 am	10:30 am
11:00 am	11:30 am
12:00 pm	12:30 pm
1:00 pm	1:30 pm
2:00 pm	2:30 pm
3:00 pm	3:30 pm
4:00 pm	4:30 pm
5:00 pm	5:30 pm
6:00 pm	6:30 pm
7:00 pm	7:30 pm
8:00 pm	8:30 pm
9:00 pm	9:30 pm

DAY / DATE ______________________________

MY GOALS TODAY

____
____
____
____
____
____

NOTES

TIME BLOCKS

3:00 am	3:30 am
4:00 am	4:30 am
5:00 am	5:30 am
6:00 am	6:30 am
7:00 am	7:30 am
8:00 am	8:30 am
9:00 am	9:30 am
10:00 am	10:30 am
11:00 am	11:30 am
12:00 pm	12:30 pm
1:00 pm	1:30 pm
2:00 pm	2:30 pm
3:00 pm	3:30 pm
4:00 pm	4:30 pm
5:00 pm	5:30 pm
6:00 pm	6:30 pm
7:00 pm	7:30 pm
8:00 pm	8:30 pm
9:00 pm	9:30 pm

DAY / DATE ______________________________

MY GOALS TODAY

____
____
____
____
____
____

NOTES

TIME BLOCKS

3:00 am	3:30 am
4:00 am	4:30 am
5:00 am	5:30 am
6:00 am	6:30 am
7:00 am	7:30 am
8:00 am	8:30 am
9:00 am	9:30 am
10:00 am	10:30 am
11:00 am	11:30 am
12:00 pm	12:30 pm
1:00 pm	1:30 pm
2:00 pm	2:30 pm
3:00 pm	3:30 pm
4:00 pm	4:30 pm
5:00 pm	5:30 pm
6:00 pm	6:30 pm
7:00 pm	7:30 pm
8:00 pm	8:30 pm
9:00 pm	9:30 pm

DAY / DATE ______________________________

MY GOALS TODAY

____

____

____

____

____

____

NOTES

TIME BLOCKS

3:00 am	3:30 am
4:00 am	4:30 am
5:00 am	5:30 am
6:00 am	6:30 am
7:00 am	7:30 am
8:00 am	8:30 am
9:00 am	9:30 am
10:00 am	10:30 am
11:00 am	11:30 am
12:00 pm	12:30 pm
1:00 pm	1:30 pm
2:00 pm	2:30 pm
3:00 pm	3:30 pm
4:00 pm	4:30 pm
5:00 pm	5:30 pm
6:00 pm	6:30 pm
7:00 pm	7:30 pm
8:00 pm	8:30 pm
9:00 pm	9:30 pm

DAY / DATE ______________________________

MY GOALS TODAY

____

____

____

____

____

____

NOTES

TIME BLOCKS

3:00 am	3:30 am
4:00 am	4:30 am
5:00 am	5:30 am
6:00 am	6:30 am
7:00 am	7:30 am
8:00 am	8:30 am
9:00 am	9:30 am
10:00 am	10:30 am
11:00 am	11:30 am
12:00 pm	12:30 pm
1:00 pm	1:30 pm
2:00 pm	2:30 pm
3:00 pm	3:30 pm
4:00 pm	4:30 pm
5:00 pm	5:30 pm
6:00 pm	6:30 pm
7:00 pm	7:30 pm
8:00 pm	8:30 pm
9:00 pm	9:30 pm

DAY / DATE ______________________________

MY GOALS TODAY

____

____

____

____

____

____

NOTES

TIME BLOCKS

3:00 am	3:30 am
4:00 am	4:30 am
5:00 am	5:30 am
6:00 am	6:30 am
7:00 am	7:30 am
8:00 am	8:30 am
9:00 am	9:30 am
10:00 am	10:30 am
11:00 am	11:30 am
12:00 pm	12:30 pm
1:00 pm	1:30 pm
2:00 pm	2:30 pm
3:00 pm	3:30 pm
4:00 pm	4:30 pm
5:00 pm	5:30 pm
6:00 pm	6:30 pm
7:00 pm	7:30 pm
8:00 pm	8:30 pm
9:00 pm	9:30 pm

DAY / DATE ____________________

MY GOALS TODAY

____

____

____

____

____

____

NOTES

TIME BLOCKS

3:00 am	3:30 am
4:00 am	4:30 am
5:00 am	5:30 am
6:00 am	6:30 am
7:00 am	7:30 am
8:00 am	8:30 am
9:00 am	9:30 am
10:00 am	10:30 am
11:00 am	11:30 am
12:00 pm	12:30 pm
1:00 pm	1:30 pm
2:00 pm	2:30 pm
3:00 pm	3:30 pm
4:00 pm	4:30 pm
5:00 pm	5:30 pm
6:00 pm	6:30 pm
7:00 pm	7:30 pm
8:00 pm	8:30 pm
9:00 pm	9:30 pm

TIME MASTERY AND BLOCKER

DAY / DATE ______________________________

MY GOALS TODAY

____

____

____

____

____

____

NOTES

TIME BLOCKS

3:00 am	3:30 am
4:00 am	4:30 am
5:00 am	5:30 am
6:00 am	6:30 am
7:00 am	7:30 am
8:00 am	8:30 am
9:00 am	9:30 am
10:00 am	10:30 am
11:00 am	11:30 am
12:00 pm	12:30 pm
1:00 pm	1:30 pm
2:00 pm	2:30 pm
3:00 pm	3:30 pm
4:00 pm	4:30 pm
5:00 pm	5:30 pm
6:00 pm	6:30 pm
7:00 pm	7:30 pm
8:00 pm	8:30 pm
9:00 pm	9:30 pm

DAY / DATE ______________________________

MY GOALS TODAY

____

____

____

____

____

____

NOTES

TIME BLOCKS

3:00 am	3:30 am
4:00 am	4:30 am
5:00 am	5:30 am
6:00 am	6:30 am
7:00 am	7:30 am
8:00 am	8:30 am
9:00 am	9:30 am
10:00 am	10:30 am
11:00 am	11:30 am
12:00 pm	12:30 pm
1:00 pm	1:30 pm
2:00 pm	2:30 pm
3:00 pm	3:30 pm
4:00 pm	4:30 pm
5:00 pm	5:30 pm
6:00 pm	6:30 pm
7:00 pm	7:30 pm
8:00 pm	8:30 pm
9:00 pm	9:30 pm

TIME MASTERY AND BLOCKER

DAY / DATE ______________________________

MY GOALS TODAY

____

____

____

____

____

____

NOTES

TIME BLOCKS

3:00 am	3:30 am
4:00 am	4:30 am
5:00 am	5:30 am
6:00 am	6:30 am
7:00 am	7:30 am
8:00 am	8:30 am
9:00 am	9:30 am
10:00 am	10:30 am
11:00 am	11:30 am
12:00 pm	12:30 pm
1:00 pm	1:30 pm
2:00 pm	2:30 pm
3:00 pm	3:30 pm
4:00 pm	4:30 pm
5:00 pm	5:30 pm
6:00 pm	6:30 pm
7:00 pm	7:30 pm
8:00 pm	8:30 pm
9:00 pm	9:30 pm

DAY / DATE ____________________

MY GOALS TODAY

____
____
____
____
____
____

NOTES

TIME BLOCKS

3:00 am	3:30 am
4:00 am	4:30 am
5:00 am	5:30 am
6:00 am	6:30 am
7:00 am	7:30 am
8:00 am	8:30 am
9:00 am	9:30 am
10:00 am	10:30 am
11:00 am	11:30 am
12:00 pm	12:30 pm
1:00 pm	1:30 pm
2:00 pm	2:30 pm
3:00 pm	3:30 pm
4:00 pm	4:30 pm
5:00 pm	5:30 pm
6:00 pm	6:30 pm
7:00 pm	7:30 pm
8:00 pm	8:30 pm
9:00 pm	9:30 pm

DAY / DATE ______________________________

MY GOALS TODAY

____

____

____

____

____

____

NOTES

TIME BLOCKS

3:00 am	3:30 am
4:00 am	4:30 am
5:00 am	5:30 am
6:00 am	6:30 am
7:00 am	7:30 am
8:00 am	8:30 am
9:00 am	9:30 am
10:00 am	10:30 am
11:00 am	11:30 am
12:00 pm	12:30 pm
1:00 pm	1:30 pm
2:00 pm	2:30 pm
3:00 pm	3:30 pm
4:00 pm	4:30 pm
5:00 pm	5:30 pm
6:00 pm	6:30 pm
7:00 pm	7:30 pm
8:00 pm	8:30 pm
9:00 pm	9:30 pm

DAY / DATE ______________________________

MY GOALS TODAY

____
____
____
____
____
____

NOTES

TIME BLOCKS

3:00 am	3:30 am
4:00 am	4:30 am
5:00 am	5:30 am
6:00 am	6:30 am
7:00 am	7:30 am
8:00 am	8:30 am
9:00 am	9:30 am
10:00 am	10:30 am
11:00 am	11:30 am
12:00 pm	12:30 pm
1:00 pm	1:30 pm
2:00 pm	2:30 pm
3:00 pm	3:30 pm
4:00 pm	4:30 pm
5:00 pm	5:30 pm
6:00 pm	6:30 pm
7:00 pm	7:30 pm
8:00 pm	8:30 pm
9:00 pm	9:30 pm

DAY / DATE ______________________________

MY GOALS TODAY

____

____

____

____

____

____

NOTES

TIME BLOCKS

3:00 am	3:30 am
4:00 am	4:30 am
5:00 am	5:30 am
6:00 am	6:30 am
7:00 am	7:30 am
8:00 am	8:30 am
9:00 am	9:30 am
10:00 am	10:30 am
11:00 am	11:30 am
12:00 pm	12:30 pm
1:00 pm	1:30 pm
2:00 pm	2:30 pm
3:00 pm	3:30 pm
4:00 pm	4:30 pm
5:00 pm	5:30 pm
6:00 pm	6:30 pm
7:00 pm	7:30 pm
8:00 pm	8:30 pm
9:00 pm	9:30 pm

DAY / DATE ______________________________

MY GOALS TODAY

____
____
____
____
____
____

NOTES

TIME BLOCKS

3:00 am	3:30 am
4:00 am	4:30 am
5:00 am	5:30 am
6:00 am	6:30 am
7:00 am	7:30 am
8:00 am	8:30 am
9:00 am	9:30 am
10:00 am	10:30 am
11:00 am	11:30 am
12:00 pm	12:30 pm
1:00 pm	1:30 pm
2:00 pm	2:30 pm
3:00 pm	3:30 pm
4:00 pm	4:30 pm
5:00 pm	5:30 pm
6:00 pm	6:30 pm
7:00 pm	7:30 pm
8:00 pm	8:30 pm
9:00 pm	9:30 pm

DAY / DATE ____________________

MY GOALS TODAY

NOTES

TIME BLOCKS

3:00 am	3:30 am
4:00 am	4:30 am
5:00 am	5:30 am
6:00 am	6:30 am
7:00 am	7:30 am
8:00 am	8:30 am
9:00 am	9:30 am
10:00 am	10:30 am
11:00 am	11:30 am
12:00 pm	12:30 pm
1:00 pm	1:30 pm
2:00 pm	2:30 pm
3:00 pm	3:30 pm
4:00 pm	4:30 pm
5:00 pm	5:30 pm
6:00 pm	6:30 pm
7:00 pm	7:30 pm
8:00 pm	8:30 pm
9:00 pm	9:30 pm

DAY / DATE ______________________________

MY GOALS TODAY

____
____
____
____
____
____

NOTES

TIME BLOCKS

3:00 am	3:30 am
4:00 am	4:30 am
5:00 am	5:30 am
6:00 am	6:30 am
7:00 am	7:30 am
8:00 am	8:30 am
9:00 am	9:30 am
10:00 am	10:30 am
11:00 am	11:30 am
12:00 pm	12:30 pm
1:00 pm	1:30 pm
2:00 pm	2:30 pm
3:00 pm	3:30 pm
4:00 pm	4:30 pm
5:00 pm	5:30 pm
6:00 pm	6:30 pm
7:00 pm	7:30 pm
8:00 pm	8:30 pm
9:00 pm	9:30 pm

DAY / DATE ______________________________

MY GOALS TODAY

____
____
____
____
____
____

NOTES

TIME BLOCKS

3:00 am	3:30 am
4:00 am	4:30 am
5:00 am	5:30 am
6:00 am	6:30 am
7:00 am	7:30 am
8:00 am	8:30 am
9:00 am	9:30 am
10:00 am	10:30 am
11:00 am	11:30 am
12:00 pm	12:30 pm
1:00 pm	1:30 pm
2:00 pm	2:30 pm
3:00 pm	3:30 pm
4:00 pm	4:30 pm
5:00 pm	5:30 pm
6:00 pm	6:30 pm
7:00 pm	7:30 pm
8:00 pm	8:30 pm
9:00 pm	9:30 pm

DAY / DATE ______________________________

MY GOALS TODAY

____
____
____
____
____
____

TIME BLOCKS

3:00 am	3:30 am
4:00 am	4:30 am
5:00 am	5:30 am
6:00 am	6:30 am
7:00 am	7:30 am
8:00 am	8:30 am
9:00 am	9:30 am
10:00 am	10:30 am
11:00 am	11:30 am
12:00 pm	12:30 pm
1:00 pm	1:30 pm
2:00 pm	2:30 pm
3:00 pm	3:30 pm
4:00 pm	4:30 pm
5:00 pm	5:30 pm
6:00 pm	6:30 pm
7:00 pm	7:30 pm
8:00 pm	8:30 pm
9:00 pm	9:30 pm

NOTES

TIME MASTERY AND BLOCKER

DAY / DATE ______________________________

MY GOALS TODAY

____

____

____

____

____

____

NOTES

TIME BLOCKS

3:00 am	3:30 am
4:00 am	4:30 am
5:00 am	5:30 am
6:00 am	6:30 am
7:00 am	7:30 am
8:00 am	8:30 am
9:00 am	9:30 am
10:00 am	10:30 am
11:00 am	11:30 am
12:00 pm	12:30 pm
1:00 pm	1:30 pm
2:00 pm	2:30 pm
3:00 pm	3:30 pm
4:00 pm	4:30 pm
5:00 pm	5:30 pm
6:00 pm	6:30 pm
7:00 pm	7:30 pm
8:00 pm	8:30 pm
9:00 pm	9:30 pm

DAY / DATE ______________________________

MY GOALS TODAY

____

____

____

____

____

____

NOTES

TIME BLOCKS

3:00 am	3:30 am
4:00 am	4:30 am
5:00 am	5:30 am
6:00 am	6:30 am
7:00 am	7:30 am
8:00 am	8:30 am
9:00 am	9:30 am
10:00 am	10:30 am
11:00 am	11:30 am
12:00 pm	12:30 pm
1:00 pm	1:30 pm
2:00 pm	2:30 pm
3:00 pm	3:30 pm
4:00 pm	4:30 pm
5:00 pm	5:30 pm
6:00 pm	6:30 pm
7:00 pm	7:30 pm
8:00 pm	8:30 pm
9:00 pm	9:30 pm

DAY / DATE ______________________________

MY GOALS TODAY

____
____
____
____
____
____

NOTES

TIME BLOCKS

3:00 am	3:30 am
4:00 am	4:30 am
5:00 am	5:30 am
6:00 am	6:30 am
7:00 am	7:30 am
8:00 am	8:30 am
9:00 am	9:30 am
10:00 am	10:30 am
11:00 am	11:30 am
12:00 pm	12:30 pm
1:00 pm	1:30 pm
2:00 pm	2:30 pm
3:00 pm	3:30 pm
4:00 pm	4:30 pm
5:00 pm	5:30 pm
6:00 pm	6:30 pm
7:00 pm	7:30 pm
8:00 pm	8:30 pm
9:00 pm	9:30 pm

DAY / DATE ______________________________

MY GOALS TODAY

____

____

____

____

____

____

NOTES

TIME BLOCKS

3:00 am	3:30 am
4:00 am	4:30 am
5:00 am	5:30 am
6:00 am	6:30 am
7:00 am	7:30 am
8:00 am	8:30 am
9:00 am	9:30 am
10:00 am	10:30 am
11:00 am	11:30 am
12:00 pm	12:30 pm
1:00 pm	1:30 pm
2:00 pm	2:30 pm
3:00 pm	3:30 pm
4:00 pm	4:30 pm
5:00 pm	5:30 pm
6:00 pm	6:30 pm
7:00 pm	7:30 pm
8:00 pm	8:30 pm
9:00 pm	9:30 pm

DAY / DATE ______________________________

MY GOALS TODAY

____

____

____

____

____

____

NOTES

TIME BLOCKS

3:00 am	3:30 am
4:00 am	4:30 am
5:00 am	5:30 am
6:00 am	6:30 am
7:00 am	7:30 am
8:00 am	8:30 am
9:00 am	9:30 am
10:00 am	10:30 am
11:00 am	11:30 am
12:00 pm	12:30 pm
1:00 pm	1:30 pm
2:00 pm	2:30 pm
3:00 pm	3:30 pm
4:00 pm	4:30 pm
5:00 pm	5:30 pm
6:00 pm	6:30 pm
7:00 pm	7:30 pm
8:00 pm	8:30 pm
9:00 pm	9:30 pm

DAY / DATE ____________________

MY GOALS TODAY

____
____
____
____
____
____

NOTES

TIME BLOCKS

3:00 am	3:30 am
4:00 am	4:30 am
5:00 am	5:30 am
6:00 am	6:30 am
7:00 am	7:30 am
8:00 am	8:30 am
9:00 am	9:30 am
10:00 am	10:30 am
11:00 am	11:30 am
12:00 pm	12:30 pm
1:00 pm	1:30 pm
2:00 pm	2:30 pm
3:00 pm	3:30 pm
4:00 pm	4:30 pm
5:00 pm	5:30 pm
6:00 pm	6:30 pm
7:00 pm	7:30 pm
8:00 pm	8:30 pm
9:00 pm	9:30 pm

DAY / DATE ______________________________

MY GOALS TODAY

____
____
____
____
____
____

NOTES

TIME BLOCKS

3:00 am	3:30 am
4:00 am	4:30 am
5:00 am	5:30 am
6:00 am	6:30 am
7:00 am	7:30 am
8:00 am	8:30 am
9:00 am	9:30 am
10:00 am	10:30 am
11:00 am	11:30 am
12:00 pm	12:30 pm
1:00 pm	1:30 pm
2:00 pm	2:30 pm
3:00 pm	3:30 pm
4:00 pm	4:30 pm
5:00 pm	5:30 pm
6:00 pm	6:30 pm
7:00 pm	7:30 pm
8:00 pm	8:30 pm
9:00 pm	9:30 pm

DAY / DATE ______________________________

MY GOALS TODAY

____

____

____

____

____

____

NOTES

TIME BLOCKS

3:00 am	3:30 am
4:00 am	4:30 am
5:00 am	5:30 am
6:00 am	6:30 am
7:00 am	7:30 am
8:00 am	8:30 am
9:00 am	9:30 am
10:00 am	10:30 am
11:00 am	11:30 am
12:00 pm	12:30 pm
1:00 pm	1:30 pm
2:00 pm	2:30 pm
3:00 pm	3:30 pm
4:00 pm	4:30 pm
5:00 pm	5:30 pm
6:00 pm	6:30 pm
7:00 pm	7:30 pm
8:00 pm	8:30 pm
9:00 pm	9:30 pm

DAY / DATE ______________________________

MY GOALS TODAY

____

____

____

____

____

____

TIME BLOCKS

3:00 am	3:30 am
4:00 am	4:30 am
5:00 am	5:30 am
6:00 am	6:30 am
7:00 am	7:30 am
8:00 am	8:30 am
9:00 am	9:30 am
10:00 am	10:30 am
11:00 am	11:30 am
12:00 pm	12:30 pm
1:00 pm	1:30 pm
2:00 pm	2:30 pm
3:00 pm	3:30 pm
4:00 pm	4:30 pm
5:00 pm	5:30 pm
6:00 pm	6:30 pm
7:00 pm	7:30 pm
8:00 pm	8:30 pm
9:00 pm	9:30 pm

NOTES

DAY / DATE ______________________________

MY GOALS TODAY

____

____

____

____

____

____

NOTES

TIME BLOCKS

3:00 am	3:30 am
4:00 am	4:30 am
5:00 am	5:30 am
6:00 am	6:30 am
7:00 am	7:30 am
8:00 am	8:30 am
9:00 am	9:30 am
10:00 am	10:30 am
11:00 am	11:30 am
12:00 pm	12:30 pm
1:00 pm	1:30 pm
2:00 pm	2:30 pm
3:00 pm	3:30 pm
4:00 pm	4:30 pm
5:00 pm	5:30 pm
6:00 pm	6:30 pm
7:00 pm	7:30 pm
8:00 pm	8:30 pm
9:00 pm	9:30 pm

DAY / DATE ______________________________

MY GOALS TODAY

____
____
____
____
____
____

NOTES

TIME BLOCKS

3:00 am	3:30 am
4:00 am	4:30 am
5:00 am	5:30 am
6:00 am	6:30 am
7:00 am	7:30 am
8:00 am	8:30 am
9:00 am	9:30 am
10:00 am	10:30 am
11:00 am	11:30 am
12:00 pm	12:30 pm
1:00 pm	1:30 pm
2:00 pm	2:30 pm
3:00 pm	3:30 pm
4:00 pm	4:30 pm
5:00 pm	5:30 pm
6:00 pm	6:30 pm
7:00 pm	7:30 pm
8:00 pm	8:30 pm
9:00 pm	9:30 pm

DAY / DATE ______________________________

MY GOALS TODAY

____

____

____

____

____

____

NOTES

TIME BLOCKS

3:00 am	3:30 am
4:00 am	4:30 am
5:00 am	5:30 am
6:00 am	6:30 am
7:00 am	7:30 am
8:00 am	8:30 am
9:00 am	9:30 am
10:00 am	10:30 am
11:00 am	11:30 am
12:00 pm	12:30 pm
1:00 pm	1:30 pm
2:00 pm	2:30 pm
3:00 pm	3:30 pm
4:00 pm	4:30 pm
5:00 pm	5:30 pm
6:00 pm	6:30 pm
7:00 pm	7:30 pm
8:00 pm	8:30 pm
9:00 pm	9:30 pm

DAY / DATE ______________________________

MY GOALS TODAY

____
____
____
____
____
____

NOTES

TIME BLOCKS

3:00 am	3:30 am
4:00 am	4:30 am
5:00 am	5:30 am
6:00 am	6:30 am
7:00 am	7:30 am
8:00 am	8:30 am
9:00 am	9:30 am
10:00 am	10:30 am
11:00 am	11:30 am
12:00 pm	12:30 pm
1:00 pm	1:30 pm
2:00 pm	2:30 pm
3:00 pm	3:30 pm
4:00 pm	4:30 pm
5:00 pm	5:30 pm
6:00 pm	6:30 pm
7:00 pm	7:30 pm
8:00 pm	8:30 pm
9:00 pm	9:30 pm

DAY / DATE ______________________________

MY GOALS TODAY

____

____

____

____

____

____

NOTES

TIME BLOCKS

3:00 am	3:30 am
4:00 am	4:30 am
5:00 am	5:30 am
6:00 am	6:30 am
7:00 am	7:30 am
8:00 am	8:30 am
9:00 am	9:30 am
10:00 am	10:30 am
11:00 am	11:30 am
12:00 pm	12:30 pm
1:00 pm	1:30 pm
2:00 pm	2:30 pm
3:00 pm	3:30 pm
4:00 pm	4:30 pm
5:00 pm	5:30 pm
6:00 pm	6:30 pm
7:00 pm	7:30 pm
8:00 pm	8:30 pm
9:00 pm	9:30 pm

DAY / DATE ______________________________

MY GOALS TODAY

____

____

____

____

____

____

TIME BLOCKS

3:00 am	3:30 am
4:00 am	4:30 am
5:00 am	5:30 am
6:00 am	6:30 am
7:00 am	7:30 am
8:00 am	8:30 am
9:00 am	9:30 am
10:00 am	10:30 am
11:00 am	11:30 am
12:00 pm	12:30 pm
1:00 pm	1:30 pm
2:00 pm	2:30 pm
3:00 pm	3:30 pm
4:00 pm	4:30 pm
5:00 pm	5:30 pm
6:00 pm	6:30 pm
7:00 pm	7:30 pm
8:00 pm	8:30 pm
9:00 pm	9:30 pm

NOTES

TIME MASTERY AND BLOCKER

DAY / DATE ______________________________

MY GOALS TODAY

____

____

____

____

____

____

NOTES

TIME BLOCKS

3:00 am	3:30 am
4:00 am	4:30 am
5:00 am	5:30 am
6:00 am	6:30 am
7:00 am	7:30 am
8:00 am	8:30 am
9:00 am	9:30 am
10:00 am	10:30 am
11:00 am	11:30 am
12:00 pm	12:30 pm
1:00 pm	1:30 pm
2:00 pm	2:30 pm
3:00 pm	3:30 pm
4:00 pm	4:30 pm
5:00 pm	5:30 pm
6:00 pm	6:30 pm
7:00 pm	7:30 pm
8:00 pm	8:30 pm
9:00 pm	9:30 pm

DAY / DATE ____________________

MY GOALS TODAY

____

____

____

____

____

____

NOTES

TIME BLOCKS

3:00 am	3:30 am
4:00 am	4:30 am
5:00 am	5:30 am
6:00 am	6:30 am
7:00 am	7:30 am
8:00 am	8:30 am
9:00 am	9:30 am
10:00 am	10:30 am
11:00 am	11:30 am
12:00 pm	12:30 pm
1:00 pm	1:30 pm
2:00 pm	2:30 pm
3:00 pm	3:30 pm
4:00 pm	4:30 pm
5:00 pm	5:30 pm
6:00 pm	6:30 pm
7:00 pm	7:30 pm
8:00 pm	8:30 pm
9:00 pm	9:30 pm

DAY / DATE ______________________________

MY GOALS TODAY

____
____
____
____
____
____

NOTES

TIME BLOCKS

3:00 am	3:30 am
4:00 am	4:30 am
5:00 am	5:30 am
6:00 am	6:30 am
7:00 am	7:30 am
8:00 am	8:30 am
9:00 am	9:30 am
10:00 am	10:30 am
11:00 am	11:30 am
12:00 pm	12:30 pm
1:00 pm	1:30 pm
2:00 pm	2:30 pm
3:00 pm	3:30 pm
4:00 pm	4:30 pm
5:00 pm	5:30 pm
6:00 pm	6:30 pm
7:00 pm	7:30 pm
8:00 pm	8:30 pm
9:00 pm	9:30 pm

DAY / DATE ______________________________

MY GOALS TODAY

____
____
____
____
____
____

NOTES

TIME BLOCKS

3:00 am	3:30 am
4:00 am	4:30 am
5:00 am	5:30 am
6:00 am	6:30 am
7:00 am	7:30 am
8:00 am	8:30 am
9:00 am	9:30 am
10:00 am	10:30 am
11:00 am	11:30 am
12:00 pm	12:30 pm
1:00 pm	1:30 pm
2:00 pm	2:30 pm
3:00 pm	3:30 pm
4:00 pm	4:30 pm
5:00 pm	5:30 pm
6:00 pm	6:30 pm
7:00 pm	7:30 pm
8:00 pm	8:30 pm
9:00 pm	9:30 pm

DAY / DATE ______________________________

MY GOALS TODAY

____

____

____

____

____

____

NOTES

TIME BLOCKS

3:00 am	3:30 am
4:00 am	4:30 am
5:00 am	5:30 am
6:00 am	6:30 am
7:00 am	7:30 am
8:00 am	8:30 am
9:00 am	9:30 am
10:00 am	10:30 am
11:00 am	11:30 am
12:00 pm	12:30 pm
1:00 pm	1:30 pm
2:00 pm	2:30 pm
3:00 pm	3:30 pm
4:00 pm	4:30 pm
5:00 pm	5:30 pm
6:00 pm	6:30 pm
7:00 pm	7:30 pm
8:00 pm	8:30 pm
9:00 pm	9:30 pm

DAY / DATE ____________________

MY GOALS TODAY

____

____

____

____

____

____

NOTES

TIME BLOCKS

3:00 am	3:30 am
4:00 am	4:30 am
5:00 am	5:30 am
6:00 am	6:30 am
7:00 am	7:30 am
8:00 am	8:30 am
9:00 am	9:30 am
10:00 am	10:30 am
11:00 am	11:30 am
12:00 pm	12:30 pm
1:00 pm	1:30 pm
2:00 pm	2:30 pm
3:00 pm	3:30 pm
4:00 pm	4:30 pm
5:00 pm	5:30 pm
6:00 pm	6:30 pm
7:00 pm	7:30 pm
8:00 pm	8:30 pm
9:00 pm	9:30 pm

DAY / DATE ____________________

MY GOALS TODAY

____

____

____

____

____

____

NOTES

TIME BLOCKS

3:00 am	3:30 am
4:00 am	4:30 am
5:00 am	5:30 am
6:00 am	6:30 am
7:00 am	7:30 am
8:00 am	8:30 am
9:00 am	9:30 am
10:00 am	10:30 am
11:00 am	11:30 am
12:00 pm	12:30 pm
1:00 pm	1:30 pm
2:00 pm	2:30 pm
3:00 pm	3:30 pm
4:00 pm	4:30 pm
5:00 pm	5:30 pm
6:00 pm	6:30 pm
7:00 pm	7:30 pm
8:00 pm	8:30 pm
9:00 pm	9:30 pm

DAY / DATE ______________________________

MY GOALS TODAY

____

____

____

____

____

____

NOTES

TIME BLOCKS

3:00 am	3:30 am
4:00 am	4:30 am
5:00 am	5:30 am
6:00 am	6:30 am
7:00 am	7:30 am
8:00 am	8:30 am
9:00 am	9:30 am
10:00 am	10:30 am
11:00 am	11:30 am
12:00 pm	12:30 pm
1:00 pm	1:30 pm
2:00 pm	2:30 pm
3:00 pm	3:30 pm
4:00 pm	4:30 pm
5:00 pm	5:30 pm
6:00 pm	6:30 pm
7:00 pm	7:30 pm
8:00 pm	8:30 pm
9:00 pm	9:30 pm

Thoughts become words. Words become action. Actions become character. Character becomes destiny.

DAY / DATE ______________________________

MY GOALS TODAY

____

____

____

____

____

____

NOTES

TIME BLOCKS

3:00 am	3:30 am
4:00 am	4:30 am
5:00 am	5:30 am
6:00 am	6:30 am
7:00 am	7:30 am
8:00 am	8:30 am
9:00 am	9:30 am
10:00 am	10:30 am
11:00 am	11:30 am
12:00 pm	12:30 pm
1:00 pm	1:30 pm
2:00 pm	2:30 pm
3:00 pm	3:30 pm
4:00 pm	4:30 pm
5:00 pm	5:30 pm
6:00 pm	6:30 pm
7:00 pm	7:30 pm
8:00 pm	8:30 pm
9:00 pm	9:30 pm

DAY / DATE ______________________________

MY GOALS TODAY

____

____

____

____

____

____

NOTES

TIME BLOCKS

3:00 am	3:30 am
4:00 am	4:30 am
5:00 am	5:30 am
6:00 am	6:30 am
7:00 am	7:30 am
8:00 am	8:30 am
9:00 am	9:30 am
10:00 am	10:30 am
11:00 am	11:30 am
12:00 pm	12:30 pm
1:00 pm	1:30 pm
2:00 pm	2:30 pm
3:00 pm	3:30 pm
4:00 pm	4:30 pm
5:00 pm	5:30 pm
6:00 pm	6:30 pm
7:00 pm	7:30 pm
8:00 pm	8:30 pm
9:00 pm	9:30 pm

Thoughts become words. Words become action. Actions become character. Character becomes destiny.

DAY / DATE ______________________________

MY GOALS TODAY

____
____
____
____
____
____

NOTES

TIME BLOCKS

3:00 am	3:30 am
4:00 am	4:30 am
5:00 am	5:30 am
6:00 am	6:30 am
7:00 am	7:30 am
8:00 am	8:30 am
9:00 am	9:30 am
10:00 am	10:30 am
11:00 am	11:30 am
12:00 pm	12:30 pm
1:00 pm	1:30 pm
2:00 pm	2:30 pm
3:00 pm	3:30 pm
4:00 pm	4:30 pm
5:00 pm	5:30 pm
6:00 pm	6:30 pm
7:00 pm	7:30 pm
8:00 pm	8:30 pm
9:00 pm	9:30 pm

DAY / DATE ____________________

MY GOALS TODAY

____
____
____
____
____
____

NOTES

TIME BLOCKS

3:00 am	3:30 am
4:00 am	4:30 am
5:00 am	5:30 am
6:00 am	6:30 am
7:00 am	7:30 am
8:00 am	8:30 am
9:00 am	9:30 am
10:00 am	10:30 am
11:00 am	11:30 am
12:00 pm	12:30 pm
1:00 pm	1:30 pm
2:00 pm	2:30 pm
3:00 pm	3:30 pm
4:00 pm	4:30 pm
5:00 pm	5:30 pm
6:00 pm	6:30 pm
7:00 pm	7:30 pm
8:00 pm	8:30 pm
9:00 pm	9:30 pm

DAY / DATE ______________________________

MY GOALS TODAY

____

____

____

____

____

____

NOTES

TIME BLOCKS

3:00 am	3:30 am
4:00 am	4:30 am
5:00 am	5:30 am
6:00 am	6:30 am
7:00 am	7:30 am
8:00 am	8:30 am
9:00 am	9:30 am
10:00 am	10:30 am
11:00 am	11:30 am
12:00 pm	12:30 pm
1:00 pm	1:30 pm
2:00 pm	2:30 pm
3:00 pm	3:30 pm
4:00 pm	4:30 pm
5:00 pm	5:30 pm
6:00 pm	6:30 pm
7:00 pm	7:30 pm
8:00 pm	8:30 pm
9:00 pm	9:30 pm

TIME MASTERY AND BLOCKER

DAY / DATE ______________________________

MY GOALS TODAY

____

____

____

____

____

____

NOTES

TIME BLOCKS

3:00 am	3:30 am
4:00 am	4:30 am
5:00 am	5:30 am
6:00 am	6:30 am
7:00 am	7:30 am
8:00 am	8:30 am
9:00 am	9:30 am
10:00 am	10:30 am
11:00 am	11:30 am
12:00 pm	12:30 pm
1:00 pm	1:30 pm
2:00 pm	2:30 pm
3:00 pm	3:30 pm
4:00 pm	4:30 pm
5:00 pm	5:30 pm
6:00 pm	6:30 pm
7:00 pm	7:30 pm
8:00 pm	8:30 pm
9:00 pm	9:30 pm

Thoughts become words. Words become action. Actions become character. Character becomes destiny.

DAY / DATE ______________________________

MY GOALS TODAY

____

____

____

____

____

____

NOTES

TIME BLOCKS

3:00 am	3:30 am
4:00 am	4:30 am
5:00 am	5:30 am
6:00 am	6:30 am
7:00 am	7:30 am
8:00 am	8:30 am
9:00 am	9:30 am
10:00 am	10:30 am
11:00 am	11:30 am
12:00 pm	12:30 pm
1:00 pm	1:30 pm
2:00 pm	2:30 pm
3:00 pm	3:30 pm
4:00 pm	4:30 pm
5:00 pm	5:30 pm
6:00 pm	6:30 pm
7:00 pm	7:30 pm
8:00 pm	8:30 pm
9:00 pm	9:30 pm

DAY / DATE ____________________

MY GOALS TODAY

____

____

____

____

____

____

NOTES

TIME BLOCKS

3:00 am	3:30 am
4:00 am	4:30 am
5:00 am	5:30 am
6:00 am	6:30 am
7:00 am	7:30 am
8:00 am	8:30 am
9:00 am	9:30 am
10:00 am	10:30 am
11:00 am	11:30 am
12:00 pm	12:30 pm
1:00 pm	1:30 pm
2:00 pm	2:30 pm
3:00 pm	3:30 pm
4:00 pm	4:30 pm
5:00 pm	5:30 pm
6:00 pm	6:30 pm
7:00 pm	7:30 pm
8:00 pm	8:30 pm
9:00 pm	9:30 pm

DAY / DATE ______________________________

MY GOALS TODAY

____
____
____
____
____
____

NOTES

TIME BLOCKS

3:00 am	3:30 am
4:00 am	4:30 am
5:00 am	5:30 am
6:00 am	6:30 am
7:00 am	7:30 am
8:00 am	8:30 am
9:00 am	9:30 am
10:00 am	10:30 am
11:00 am	11:30 am
12:00 pm	12:30 pm
1:00 pm	1:30 pm
2:00 pm	2:30 pm
3:00 pm	3:30 pm
4:00 pm	4:30 pm
5:00 pm	5:30 pm
6:00 pm	6:30 pm
7:00 pm	7:30 pm
8:00 pm	8:30 pm
9:00 pm	9:30 pm

DAY / DATE ______________________________

MY GOALS TODAY

____
____
____
____
____
____

NOTES

TIME BLOCKS

3:00 am	3:30 am
4:00 am	4:30 am
5:00 am	5:30 am
6:00 am	6:30 am
7:00 am	7:30 am
8:00 am	8:30 am
9:00 am	9:30 am
10:00 am	10:30 am
11:00 am	11:30 am
12:00 pm	12:30 pm
1:00 pm	1:30 pm
2:00 pm	2:30 pm
3:00 pm	3:30 pm
4:00 pm	4:30 pm
5:00 pm	5:30 pm
6:00 pm	6:30 pm
7:00 pm	7:30 pm
8:00 pm	8:30 pm
9:00 pm	9:30 pm

DAY / DATE ______________________________

MY GOALS TODAY

____
____
____
____
____
____

NOTES

TIME BLOCKS

3:00 am	3:30 am
4:00 am	4:30 am
5:00 am	5:30 am
6:00 am	6:30 am
7:00 am	7:30 am
8:00 am	8:30 am
9:00 am	9:30 am
10:00 am	10:30 am
11:00 am	11:30 am
12:00 pm	12:30 pm
1:00 pm	1:30 pm
2:00 pm	2:30 pm
3:00 pm	3:30 pm
4:00 pm	4:30 pm
5:00 pm	5:30 pm
6:00 pm	6:30 pm
7:00 pm	7:30 pm
8:00 pm	8:30 pm
9:00 pm	9:30 pm

DAY / DATE ______________________________

MY GOALS TODAY

____

____

____

____

____

____

NOTES

TIME BLOCKS

3:00 am	3:30 am
4:00 am	4:30 am
5:00 am	5:30 am
6:00 am	6:30 am
7:00 am	7:30 am
8:00 am	8:30 am
9:00 am	9:30 am
10:00 am	10:30 am
11:00 am	11:30 am
12:00 pm	12:30 pm
1:00 pm	1:30 pm
2:00 pm	2:30 pm
3:00 pm	3:30 pm
4:00 pm	4:30 pm
5:00 pm	5:30 pm
6:00 pm	6:30 pm
7:00 pm	7:30 pm
8:00 pm	8:30 pm
9:00 pm	9:30 pm

DAY / DATE ______________________

MY GOALS TODAY

____
____
____
____
____
____

NOTES

TIME BLOCKS

3:00 am	3:30 am
4:00 am	4:30 am
5:00 am	5:30 am
6:00 am	6:30 am
7:00 am	7:30 am
8:00 am	8:30 am
9:00 am	9:30 am
10:00 am	10:30 am
11:00 am	11:30 am
12:00 pm	12:30 pm
1:00 pm	1:30 pm
2:00 pm	2:30 pm
3:00 pm	3:30 pm
4:00 pm	4:30 pm
5:00 pm	5:30 pm
6:00 pm	6:30 pm
7:00 pm	7:30 pm
8:00 pm	8:30 pm
9:00 pm	9:30 pm

TIME MASTERY AND BLOCKER

DAY / DATE ______________________________

MY GOALS TODAY

____

____

____

____

____

____

NOTES

TIME BLOCKS

3:00 am	3:30 am
4:00 am	4:30 am
5:00 am	5:30 am
6:00 am	6:30 am
7:00 am	7:30 am
8:00 am	8:30 am
9:00 am	9:30 am
10:00 am	10:30 am
11:00 am	11:30 am
12:00 pm	12:30 pm
1:00 pm	1:30 pm
2:00 pm	2:30 pm
3:00 pm	3:30 pm
4:00 pm	4:30 pm
5:00 pm	5:30 pm
6:00 pm	6:30 pm
7:00 pm	7:30 pm
8:00 pm	8:30 pm
9:00 pm	9:30 pm

Thoughts become words. Words become action. Actions become character. Character becomes destiny.

DAY / DATE ____________________

MY GOALS TODAY

TIME BLOCKS

3:00 am	3:30 am
4:00 am	4:30 am
5:00 am	5:30 am
6:00 am	6:30 am
7:00 am	7:30 am
8:00 am	8:30 am
9:00 am	9:30 am
10:00 am	10:30 am
11:00 am	11:30 am
12:00 pm	12:30 pm
1:00 pm	1:30 pm
2:00 pm	2:30 pm
3:00 pm	3:30 pm
4:00 pm	4:30 pm
5:00 pm	5:30 pm
6:00 pm	6:30 pm
7:00 pm	7:30 pm
8:00 pm	8:30 pm
9:00 pm	9:30 pm

NOTES

DAY / DATE ______________________________

MY GOALS TODAY

____
____
____
____
____
____

NOTES

TIME BLOCKS

3:00 am	3:30 am
4:00 am	4:30 am
5:00 am	5:30 am
6:00 am	6:30 am
7:00 am	7:30 am
8:00 am	8:30 am
9:00 am	9:30 am
10:00 am	10:30 am
11:00 am	11:30 am
12:00 pm	12:30 pm
1:00 pm	1:30 pm
2:00 pm	2:30 pm
3:00 pm	3:30 pm
4:00 pm	4:30 pm
5:00 pm	5:30 pm
6:00 pm	6:30 pm
7:00 pm	7:30 pm
8:00 pm	8:30 pm
9:00 pm	9:30 pm

DAY / DATE ______________________________

MY GOALS TODAY

____

____

____

____

____

____

NOTES

TIME BLOCKS

3:00 am	3:30 am
4:00 am	4:30 am
5:00 am	5:30 am
6:00 am	6:30 am
7:00 am	7:30 am
8:00 am	8:30 am
9:00 am	9:30 am
10:00 am	10:30 am
11:00 am	11:30 am
12:00 pm	12:30 pm
1:00 pm	1:30 pm
2:00 pm	2:30 pm
3:00 pm	3:30 pm
4:00 pm	4:30 pm
5:00 pm	5:30 pm
6:00 pm	6:30 pm
7:00 pm	7:30 pm
8:00 pm	8:30 pm
9:00 pm	9:30 pm

DAY / DATE ______________________________

MY GOALS TODAY

____

____

____

____

____

____

NOTES

TIME BLOCKS

3:00 am	3:30 am
4:00 am	4:30 am
5:00 am	5:30 am
6:00 am	6:30 am
7:00 am	7:30 am
8:00 am	8:30 am
9:00 am	9:30 am
10:00 am	10:30 am
11:00 am	11:30 am
12:00 pm	12:30 pm
1:00 pm	1:30 pm
2:00 pm	2:30 pm
3:00 pm	3:30 pm
4:00 pm	4:30 pm
5:00 pm	5:30 pm
6:00 pm	6:30 pm
7:00 pm	7:30 pm
8:00 pm	8:30 pm
9:00 pm	9:30 pm

DAY / DATE ______________________________

MY GOALS TODAY

____
____
____
____
____
____

NOTES

TIME BLOCKS

3:00 am	3:30 am
4:00 am	4:30 am
5:00 am	5:30 am
6:00 am	6:30 am
7:00 am	7:30 am
8:00 am	8:30 am
9:00 am	9:30 am
10:00 am	10:30 am
11:00 am	11:30 am
12:00 pm	12:30 pm
1:00 pm	1:30 pm
2:00 pm	2:30 pm
3:00 pm	3:30 pm
4:00 pm	4:30 pm
5:00 pm	5:30 pm
6:00 pm	6:30 pm
7:00 pm	7:30 pm
8:00 pm	8:30 pm
9:00 pm	9:30 pm

DAY / DATE ______________________________

MY GOALS TODAY

____
____
____
____
____
____

NOTES

TIME BLOCKS

3:00 am	3:30 am
4:00 am	4:30 am
5:00 am	5:30 am
6:00 am	6:30 am
7:00 am	7:30 am
8:00 am	8:30 am
9:00 am	9:30 am
10:00 am	10:30 am
11:00 am	11:30 am
12:00 pm	12:30 pm
1:00 pm	1:30 pm
2:00 pm	2:30 pm
3:00 pm	3:30 pm
4:00 pm	4:30 pm
5:00 pm	5:30 pm
6:00 pm	6:30 pm
7:00 pm	7:30 pm
8:00 pm	8:30 pm
9:00 pm	9:30 pm

DAY / DATE ______________________

MY GOALS TODAY

____
____
____
____
____
____

NOTES

TIME BLOCKS

3:00 am	3:30 am
4:00 am	4:30 am
5:00 am	5:30 am
6:00 am	6:30 am
7:00 am	7:30 am
8:00 am	8:30 am
9:00 am	9:30 am
10:00 am	10:30 am
11:00 am	11:30 am
12:00 pm	12:30 pm
1:00 pm	1:30 pm
2:00 pm	2:30 pm
3:00 pm	3:30 pm
4:00 pm	4:30 pm
5:00 pm	5:30 pm
6:00 pm	6:30 pm
7:00 pm	7:30 pm
8:00 pm	8:30 pm
9:00 pm	9:30 pm

TIME MASTERY AND BLOCKER

DAY / DATE ____________________

MY GOALS TODAY

____
____
____
____
____
____

NOTES

TIME BLOCKS

3:00 am	3:30 am
4:00 am	4:30 am
5:00 am	5:30 am
6:00 am	6:30 am
7:00 am	7:30 am
8:00 am	8:30 am
9:00 am	9:30 am
10:00 am	10:30 am
11:00 am	11:30 am
12:00 pm	12:30 pm
1:00 pm	1:30 pm
2:00 pm	2:30 pm
3:00 pm	3:30 pm
4:00 pm	4:30 pm
5:00 pm	5:30 pm
6:00 pm	6:30 pm
7:00 pm	7:30 pm
8:00 pm	8:30 pm
9:00 pm	9:30 pm

DAY / DATE ______________________________

MY GOALS TODAY

____
____
____
____
____
____

NOTES

TIME BLOCKS

3:00 am	3:30 am
4:00 am	4:30 am
5:00 am	5:30 am
6:00 am	6:30 am
7:00 am	7:30 am
8:00 am	8:30 am
9:00 am	9:30 am
10:00 am	10:30 am
11:00 am	11:30 am
12:00 pm	12:30 pm
1:00 pm	1:30 pm
2:00 pm	2:30 pm
3:00 pm	3:30 pm
4:00 pm	4:30 pm
5:00 pm	5:30 pm
6:00 pm	6:30 pm
7:00 pm	7:30 pm
8:00 pm	8:30 pm
9:00 pm	9:30 pm

DAY / DATE ______________________________

MY GOALS TODAY

____

____

____

____

____

____

NOTES

TIME BLOCKS

3:00 am	3:30 am
4:00 am	4:30 am
5:00 am	5:30 am
6:00 am	6:30 am
7:00 am	7:30 am
8:00 am	8:30 am
9:00 am	9:30 am
10:00 am	10:30 am
11:00 am	11:30 am
12:00 pm	12:30 pm
1:00 pm	1:30 pm
2:00 pm	2:30 pm
3:00 pm	3:30 pm
4:00 pm	4:30 pm
5:00 pm	5:30 pm
6:00 pm	6:30 pm
7:00 pm	7:30 pm
8:00 pm	8:30 pm
9:00 pm	9:30 pm

DAY / DATE ______________________________

MY GOALS TODAY

____

____

____

____

____

____

TIME BLOCKS

3:00 am	3:30 am
4:00 am	4:30 am
5:00 am	5:30 am
6:00 am	6:30 am
7:00 am	7:30 am
8:00 am	8:30 am
9:00 am	9:30 am
10:00 am	10:30 am
11:00 am	11:30 am
12:00 pm	12:30 pm
1:00 pm	1:30 pm
2:00 pm	2:30 pm
3:00 pm	3:30 pm
4:00 pm	4:30 pm
5:00 pm	5:30 pm
6:00 pm	6:30 pm
7:00 pm	7:30 pm
8:00 pm	8:30 pm
9:00 pm	9:30 pm

NOTES

Thoughts become words. Words become action. Actions become character. Character becomes destiny.

DAY / DATE ______________________________

MY GOALS TODAY

____
____
____
____
____
____

NOTES

TIME BLOCKS

3:00 am	3:30 am
4:00 am	4:30 am
5:00 am	5:30 am
6:00 am	6:30 am
7:00 am	7:30 am
8:00 am	8:30 am
9:00 am	9:30 am
10:00 am	10:30 am
11:00 am	11:30 am
12:00 pm	12:30 pm
1:00 pm	1:30 pm
2:00 pm	2:30 pm
3:00 pm	3:30 pm
4:00 pm	4:30 pm
5:00 pm	5:30 pm
6:00 pm	6:30 pm
7:00 pm	7:30 pm
8:00 pm	8:30 pm
9:00 pm	9:30 pm

DAY / DATE ______________________________

MY GOALS TODAY

____
____
____
____
____
____

NOTES

TIME BLOCKS

3:00 am	3:30 am
4:00 am	4:30 am
5:00 am	5:30 am
6:00 am	6:30 am
7:00 am	7:30 am
8:00 am	8:30 am
9:00 am	9:30 am
10:00 am	10:30 am
11:00 am	11:30 am
12:00 pm	12:30 pm
1:00 pm	1:30 pm
2:00 pm	2:30 pm
3:00 pm	3:30 pm
4:00 pm	4:30 pm
5:00 pm	5:30 pm
6:00 pm	6:30 pm
7:00 pm	7:30 pm
8:00 pm	8:30 pm
9:00 pm	9:30 pm

DAY / DATE ______________________________

MY GOALS TODAY

____
____
____
____
____
____

NOTES

TIME BLOCKS

3:00 am	3:30 am
4:00 am	4:30 am
5:00 am	5:30 am
6:00 am	6:30 am
7:00 am	7:30 am
8:00 am	8:30 am
9:00 am	9:30 am
10:00 am	10:30 am
11:00 am	11:30 am
12:00 pm	12:30 pm
1:00 pm	1:30 pm
2:00 pm	2:30 pm
3:00 pm	3:30 pm
4:00 pm	4:30 pm
5:00 pm	5:30 pm
6:00 pm	6:30 pm
7:00 pm	7:30 pm
8:00 pm	8:30 pm
9:00 pm	9:30 pm

DAY / DATE ______________________________

MY GOALS TODAY

____

____

____

____

____

____

NOTES

TIME BLOCKS

3:00 am	3:30 am
4:00 am	4:30 am
5:00 am	5:30 am
6:00 am	6:30 am
7:00 am	7:30 am
8:00 am	8:30 am
9:00 am	9:30 am
10:00 am	10:30 am
11:00 am	11:30 am
12:00 pm	12:30 pm
1:00 pm	1:30 pm
2:00 pm	2:30 pm
3:00 pm	3:30 pm
4:00 pm	4:30 pm
5:00 pm	5:30 pm
6:00 pm	6:30 pm
7:00 pm	7:30 pm
8:00 pm	8:30 pm
9:00 pm	9:30 pm

DAY / DATE ______________________________

MY GOALS TODAY

____
____
____
____
____
____

NOTES

TIME BLOCKS

3:00 am	3:30 am
4:00 am	4:30 am
5:00 am	5:30 am
6:00 am	6:30 am
7:00 am	7:30 am
8:00 am	8:30 am
9:00 am	9:30 am
10:00 am	10:30 am
11:00 am	11:30 am
12:00 pm	12:30 pm
1:00 pm	1:30 pm
2:00 pm	2:30 pm
3:00 pm	3:30 pm
4:00 pm	4:30 pm
5:00 pm	5:30 pm
6:00 pm	6:30 pm
7:00 pm	7:30 pm
8:00 pm	8:30 pm
9:00 pm	9:30 pm

DAY / DATE ______________________________

MY GOALS TODAY

____

____

____

____

____

____

TIME BLOCKS

3:00 am	3:30 am
4:00 am	4:30 am
5:00 am	5:30 am
6:00 am	6:30 am
7:00 am	7:30 am
8:00 am	8:30 am
9:00 am	9:30 am
10:00 am	10:30 am
11:00 am	11:30 am
12:00 pm	12:30 pm
1:00 pm	1:30 pm
2:00 pm	2:30 pm
3:00 pm	3:30 pm
4:00 pm	4:30 pm
5:00 pm	5:30 pm
6:00 pm	6:30 pm
7:00 pm	7:30 pm
8:00 pm	8:30 pm
9:00 pm	9:30 pm

NOTES

DAY / DATE ______________________________

MY GOALS TODAY

____

____

____

____

____

____

NOTES

TIME BLOCKS

3:00 am	3:30 am
4:00 am	4:30 am
5:00 am	5:30 am
6:00 am	6:30 am
7:00 am	7:30 am
8:00 am	8:30 am
9:00 am	9:30 am
10:00 am	10:30 am
11:00 am	11:30 am
12:00 pm	12:30 pm
1:00 pm	1:30 pm
2:00 pm	2:30 pm
3:00 pm	3:30 pm
4:00 pm	4:30 pm
5:00 pm	5:30 pm
6:00 pm	6:30 pm
7:00 pm	7:30 pm
8:00 pm	8:30 pm
9:00 pm	9:30 pm

DAY / DATE ______________________________

MY GOALS TODAY

____
____
____
____
____
____

NOTES

TIME BLOCKS

3:00 am	3:30 am
4:00 am	4:30 am
5:00 am	5:30 am
6:00 am	6:30 am
7:00 am	7:30 am
8:00 am	8:30 am
9:00 am	9:30 am
10:00 am	10:30 am
11:00 am	11:30 am
12:00 pm	12:30 pm
1:00 pm	1:30 pm
2:00 pm	2:30 pm
3:00 pm	3:30 pm
4:00 pm	4:30 pm
5:00 pm	5:30 pm
6:00 pm	6:30 pm
7:00 pm	7:30 pm
8:00 pm	8:30 pm
9:00 pm	9:30 pm

DAY / DATE ____________________

MY GOALS TODAY

____

____

____

____

____

____

NOTES

TIME BLOCKS

3:00 am	3:30 am
4:00 am	4:30 am
5:00 am	5:30 am
6:00 am	6:30 am
7:00 am	7:30 am
8:00 am	8:30 am
9:00 am	9:30 am
10:00 am	10:30 am
11:00 am	11:30 am
12:00 pm	12:30 pm
1:00 pm	1:30 pm
2:00 pm	2:30 pm
3:00 pm	3:30 pm
4:00 pm	4:30 pm
5:00 pm	5:30 pm
6:00 pm	6:30 pm
7:00 pm	7:30 pm
8:00 pm	8:30 pm
9:00 pm	9:30 pm

DAY / DATE ____________________

MY GOALS TODAY

____
____
____
____
____
____

NOTES

TIME BLOCKS

3:00 am	3:30 am
4:00 am	4:30 am
5:00 am	5:30 am
6:00 am	6:30 am
7:00 am	7:30 am
8:00 am	8:30 am
9:00 am	9:30 am
10:00 am	10:30 am
11:00 am	11:30 am
12:00 pm	12:30 pm
1:00 pm	1:30 pm
2:00 pm	2:30 pm
3:00 pm	3:30 pm
4:00 pm	4:30 pm
5:00 pm	5:30 pm
6:00 pm	6:30 pm
7:00 pm	7:30 pm
8:00 pm	8:30 pm
9:00 pm	9:30 pm

DAY / DATE ____________________

MY GOALS TODAY

____
____
____
____
____
____

NOTES

TIME BLOCKS

3:00 am	3:30 am
4:00 am	4:30 am
5:00 am	5:30 am
6:00 am	6:30 am
7:00 am	7:30 am
8:00 am	8:30 am
9:00 am	9:30 am
10:00 am	10:30 am
11:00 am	11:30 am
12:00 pm	12:30 pm
1:00 pm	1:30 pm
2:00 pm	2:30 pm
3:00 pm	3:30 pm
4:00 pm	4:30 pm
5:00 pm	5:30 pm
6:00 pm	6:30 pm
7:00 pm	7:30 pm
8:00 pm	8:30 pm
9:00 pm	9:30 pm

DAY / DATE ____________________

MY GOALS TODAY

____
____
____
____
____
____

NOTES

TIME BLOCKS

3:00 am	3:30 am
4:00 am	4:30 am
5:00 am	5:30 am
6:00 am	6:30 am
7:00 am	7:30 am
8:00 am	8:30 am
9:00 am	9:30 am
10:00 am	10:30 am
11:00 am	11:30 am
12:00 pm	12:30 pm
1:00 pm	1:30 pm
2:00 pm	2:30 pm
3:00 pm	3:30 pm
4:00 pm	4:30 pm
5:00 pm	5:30 pm
6:00 pm	6:30 pm
7:00 pm	7:30 pm
8:00 pm	8:30 pm
9:00 pm	9:30 pm

DAY / DATE ______________________________

MY GOALS TODAY

____

____

____

____

____

____

NOTES

TIME BLOCKS

3:00 am	3:30 am
4:00 am	4:30 am
5:00 am	5:30 am
6:00 am	6:30 am
7:00 am	7:30 am
8:00 am	8:30 am
9:00 am	9:30 am
10:00 am	10:30 am
11:00 am	11:30 am
12:00 pm	12:30 pm
1:00 pm	1:30 pm
2:00 pm	2:30 pm
3:00 pm	3:30 pm
4:00 pm	4:30 pm
5:00 pm	5:30 pm
6:00 pm	6:30 pm
7:00 pm	7:30 pm
8:00 pm	8:30 pm
9:00 pm	9:30 pm

DAY / DATE ______________________________

MY GOALS TODAY

____
____
____
____
____
____

NOTES

TIME BLOCKS

3:00 am	3:30 am
4:00 am	4:30 am
5:00 am	5:30 am
6:00 am	6:30 am
7:00 am	7:30 am
8:00 am	8:30 am
9:00 am	9:30 am
10:00 am	10:30 am
11:00 am	11:30 am
12:00 pm	12:30 pm
1:00 pm	1:30 pm
2:00 pm	2:30 pm
3:00 pm	3:30 pm
4:00 pm	4:30 pm
5:00 pm	5:30 pm
6:00 pm	6:30 pm
7:00 pm	7:30 pm
8:00 pm	8:30 pm
9:00 pm	9:30 pm

DAY / DATE ____________________

MY GOALS TODAY

____
____
____
____
____
____

NOTES

TIME BLOCKS

3:00 am	3:30 am
4:00 am	4:30 am
5:00 am	5:30 am
6:00 am	6:30 am
7:00 am	7:30 am
8:00 am	8:30 am
9:00 am	9:30 am
10:00 am	10:30 am
11:00 am	11:30 am
12:00 pm	12:30 pm
1:00 pm	1:30 pm
2:00 pm	2:30 pm
3:00 pm	3:30 pm
4:00 pm	4:30 pm
5:00 pm	5:30 pm
6:00 pm	6:30 pm
7:00 pm	7:30 pm
8:00 pm	8:30 pm
9:00 pm	9:30 pm

DAY / DATE ______________________________

MY GOALS TODAY

____

____

____

____

____

____

NOTES

TIME BLOCKS

3:00 am	3:30 am
4:00 am	4:30 am
5:00 am	5:30 am
6:00 am	6:30 am
7:00 am	7:30 am
8:00 am	8:30 am
9:00 am	9:30 am
10:00 am	10:30 am
11:00 am	11:30 am
12:00 pm	12:30 pm
1:00 pm	1:30 pm
2:00 pm	2:30 pm
3:00 pm	3:30 pm
4:00 pm	4:30 pm
5:00 pm	5:30 pm
6:00 pm	6:30 pm
7:00 pm	7:30 pm
8:00 pm	8:30 pm
9:00 pm	9:30 pm

DAY / DATE ______________________________

MY GOALS TODAY

____

____

____

____

____

____

NOTES

TIME BLOCKS

3:00 am	3:30 am
4:00 am	4:30 am
5:00 am	5:30 am
6:00 am	6:30 am
7:00 am	7:30 am
8:00 am	8:30 am
9:00 am	9:30 am
10:00 am	10:30 am
11:00 am	11:30 am
12:00 pm	12:30 pm
1:00 pm	1:30 pm
2:00 pm	2:30 pm
3:00 pm	3:30 pm
4:00 pm	4:30 pm
5:00 pm	5:30 pm
6:00 pm	6:30 pm
7:00 pm	7:30 pm
8:00 pm	8:30 pm
9:00 pm	9:30 pm

DAY / DATE ______________________________

MY GOALS TODAY

____

____

____

____

____

____

NOTES

TIME BLOCKS

3:00 am	3:30 am
4:00 am	4:30 am
5:00 am	5:30 am
6:00 am	6:30 am
7:00 am	7:30 am
8:00 am	8:30 am
9:00 am	9:30 am
10:00 am	10:30 am
11:00 am	11:30 am
12:00 pm	12:30 pm
1:00 pm	1:30 pm
2:00 pm	2:30 pm
3:00 pm	3:30 pm
4:00 pm	4:30 pm
5:00 pm	5:30 pm
6:00 pm	6:30 pm
7:00 pm	7:30 pm
8:00 pm	8:30 pm
9:00 pm	9:30 pm

DAY / DATE ______________________________

MY GOALS TODAY

____

____

____

____

____

____

NOTES

TIME BLOCKS

3:00 am	3:30 am
4:00 am	4:30 am
5:00 am	5:30 am
6:00 am	6:30 am
7:00 am	7:30 am
8:00 am	8:30 am
9:00 am	9:30 am
10:00 am	10:30 am
11:00 am	11:30 am
12:00 pm	12:30 pm
1:00 pm	1:30 pm
2:00 pm	2:30 pm
3:00 pm	3:30 pm
4:00 pm	4:30 pm
5:00 pm	5:30 pm
6:00 pm	6:30 pm
7:00 pm	7:30 pm
8:00 pm	8:30 pm
9:00 pm	9:30 pm

DAY / DATE ______________________________

MY GOALS TODAY

____
____
____
____
____
____

NOTES

TIME BLOCKS

3:00 am	3:30 am
4:00 am	4:30 am
5:00 am	5:30 am
6:00 am	6:30 am
7:00 am	7:30 am
8:00 am	8:30 am
9:00 am	9:30 am
10:00 am	10:30 am
11:00 am	11:30 am
12:00 pm	12:30 pm
1:00 pm	1:30 pm
2:00 pm	2:30 pm
3:00 pm	3:30 pm
4:00 pm	4:30 pm
5:00 pm	5:30 pm
6:00 pm	6:30 pm
7:00 pm	7:30 pm
8:00 pm	8:30 pm
9:00 pm	9:30 pm

DAY / DATE ____________________

MY GOALS TODAY

____

____

____

____

____

____

NOTES

TIME BLOCKS

3:00 am	3:30 am
4:00 am	4:30 am
5:00 am	5:30 am
6:00 am	6:30 am
7:00 am	7:30 am
8:00 am	8:30 am
9:00 am	9:30 am
10:00 am	10:30 am
11:00 am	11:30 am
12:00 pm	12:30 pm
1:00 pm	1:30 pm
2:00 pm	2:30 pm
3:00 pm	3:30 pm
4:00 pm	4:30 pm
5:00 pm	5:30 pm
6:00 pm	6:30 pm
7:00 pm	7:30 pm
8:00 pm	8:30 pm
9:00 pm	9:30 pm

DAY / DATE ______________________________

MY GOALS TODAY

____

____

____

____

____

____

NOTES

TIME BLOCKS

3:00 am	3:30 am
4:00 am	4:30 am
5:00 am	5:30 am
6:00 am	6:30 am
7:00 am	7:30 am
8:00 am	8:30 am
9:00 am	9:30 am
10:00 am	10:30 am
11:00 am	11:30 am
12:00 pm	12:30 pm
1:00 pm	1:30 pm
2:00 pm	2:30 pm
3:00 pm	3:30 pm
4:00 pm	4:30 pm
5:00 pm	5:30 pm
6:00 pm	6:30 pm
7:00 pm	7:30 pm
8:00 pm	8:30 pm
9:00 pm	9:30 pm

DAY / DATE ___________________________

MY GOALS TODAY

TIME BLOCKS

3:00 am	3:30 am
4:00 am	4:30 am
5:00 am	5:30 am
6:00 am	6:30 am
7:00 am	7:30 am
8:00 am	8:30 am
9:00 am	9:30 am
10:00 am	10:30 am
11:00 am	11:30 am
12:00 pm	12:30 pm
1:00 pm	1:30 pm
2:00 pm	2:30 pm
3:00 pm	3:30 pm
4:00 pm	4:30 pm
5:00 pm	5:30 pm
6:00 pm	6:30 pm
7:00 pm	7:30 pm
8:00 pm	8:30 pm
9:00 pm	9:30 pm

NOTES

DAY / DATE ______________________________

MY GOALS TODAY

____
____
____
____
____
____

NOTES

TIME BLOCKS

3:00 am	3:30 am
4:00 am	4:30 am
5:00 am	5:30 am
6:00 am	6:30 am
7:00 am	7:30 am
8:00 am	8:30 am
9:00 am	9:30 am
10:00 am	10:30 am
11:00 am	11:30 am
12:00 pm	12:30 pm
1:00 pm	1:30 pm
2:00 pm	2:30 pm
3:00 pm	3:30 pm
4:00 pm	4:30 pm
5:00 pm	5:30 pm
6:00 pm	6:30 pm
7:00 pm	7:30 pm
8:00 pm	8:30 pm
9:00 pm	9:30 pm

DAY / DATE ______________________________

MY GOALS TODAY

____
____
____
____
____
____

NOTES

TIME BLOCKS

3:00 am	3:30 am
4:00 am	4:30 am
5:00 am	5:30 am
6:00 am	6:30 am
7:00 am	7:30 am
8:00 am	8:30 am
9:00 am	9:30 am
10:00 am	10:30 am
11:00 am	11:30 am
12:00 pm	12:30 pm
1:00 pm	1:30 pm
2:00 pm	2:30 pm
3:00 pm	3:30 pm
4:00 pm	4:30 pm
5:00 pm	5:30 pm
6:00 pm	6:30 pm
7:00 pm	7:30 pm
8:00 pm	8:30 pm
9:00 pm	9:30 pm

DAY / DATE ______________________________

MY GOALS TODAY

____
____
____
____
____
____

NOTES

TIME BLOCKS

3:00 am	3:30 am
4:00 am	4:30 am
5:00 am	5:30 am
6:00 am	6:30 am
7:00 am	7:30 am
8:00 am	8:30 am
9:00 am	9:30 am
10:00 am	10:30 am
11:00 am	11:30 am
12:00 pm	12:30 pm
1:00 pm	1:30 pm
2:00 pm	2:30 pm
3:00 pm	3:30 pm
4:00 pm	4:30 pm
5:00 pm	5:30 pm
6:00 pm	6:30 pm
7:00 pm	7:30 pm
8:00 pm	8:30 pm
9:00 pm	9:30 pm

Thoughts become words. Words become action. Actions become character. Character becomes destiny.

DAY / DATE ____________________

MY GOALS TODAY

NOTES

TIME BLOCKS

3:00 am	3:30 am
4:00 am	4:30 am
5:00 am	5:30 am
6:00 am	6:30 am
7:00 am	7:30 am
8:00 am	8:30 am
9:00 am	9:30 am
10:00 am	10:30 am
11:00 am	11:30 am
12:00 pm	12:30 pm
1:00 pm	1:30 pm
2:00 pm	2:30 pm
3:00 pm	3:30 pm
4:00 pm	4:30 pm
5:00 pm	5:30 pm
6:00 pm	6:30 pm
7:00 pm	7:30 pm
8:00 pm	8:30 pm
9:00 pm	9:30 pm

DAY / DATE ____________________

MY GOALS TODAY

____

____

____

____

____

____

NOTES

TIME BLOCKS

3:00 am	3:30 am
4:00 am	4:30 am
5:00 am	5:30 am
6:00 am	6:30 am
7:00 am	7:30 am
8:00 am	8:30 am
9:00 am	9:30 am
10:00 am	10:30 am
11:00 am	11:30 am
12:00 pm	12:30 pm
1:00 pm	1:30 pm
2:00 pm	2:30 pm
3:00 pm	3:30 pm
4:00 pm	4:30 pm
5:00 pm	5:30 pm
6:00 pm	6:30 pm
7:00 pm	7:30 pm
8:00 pm	8:30 pm
9:00 pm	9:30 pm

DAY / DATE ______________________________

MY GOALS TODAY

____

____

____

____

____

____

NOTES

TIME BLOCKS

3:00 am	3:30 am
4:00 am	4:30 am
5:00 am	5:30 am
6:00 am	6:30 am
7:00 am	7:30 am
8:00 am	8:30 am
9:00 am	9:30 am
10:00 am	10:30 am
11:00 am	11:30 am
12:00 pm	12:30 pm
1:00 pm	1:30 pm
2:00 pm	2:30 pm
3:00 pm	3:30 pm
4:00 pm	4:30 pm
5:00 pm	5:30 pm
6:00 pm	6:30 pm
7:00 pm	7:30 pm
8:00 pm	8:30 pm
9:00 pm	9:30 pm

DAY / DATE ______________________________

MY GOALS TODAY

____

____

____

____

____

____

NOTES

TIME BLOCKS

3:00 am	3:30 am
4:00 am	4:30 am
5:00 am	5:30 am
6:00 am	6:30 am
7:00 am	7:30 am
8:00 am	8:30 am
9:00 am	9:30 am
10:00 am	10:30 am
11:00 am	11:30 am
12:00 pm	12:30 pm
1:00 pm	1:30 pm
2:00 pm	2:30 pm
3:00 pm	3:30 pm
4:00 pm	4:30 pm
5:00 pm	5:30 pm
6:00 pm	6:30 pm
7:00 pm	7:30 pm
8:00 pm	8:30 pm
9:00 pm	9:30 pm

DAY / DATE ______________________________

MY GOALS TODAY

____

____

____

____

____

____

NOTES

TIME BLOCKS

3:00 am	3:30 am
4:00 am	4:30 am
5:00 am	5:30 am
6:00 am	6:30 am
7:00 am	7:30 am
8:00 am	8:30 am
9:00 am	9:30 am
10:00 am	10:30 am
11:00 am	11:30 am
12:00 pm	12:30 pm
1:00 pm	1:30 pm
2:00 pm	2:30 pm
3:00 pm	3:30 pm
4:00 pm	4:30 pm
5:00 pm	5:30 pm
6:00 pm	6:30 pm
7:00 pm	7:30 pm
8:00 pm	8:30 pm
9:00 pm	9:30 pm

DAY / DATE ____________________

MY GOALS TODAY

____

____

____

____

____

____

NOTES

TIME BLOCKS

3:00 am	3:30 am
4:00 am	4:30 am
5:00 am	5:30 am
6:00 am	6:30 am
7:00 am	7:30 am
8:00 am	8:30 am
9:00 am	9:30 am
10:00 am	10:30 am
11:00 am	11:30 am
12:00 pm	12:30 pm
1:00 pm	1:30 pm
2:00 pm	2:30 pm
3:00 pm	3:30 pm
4:00 pm	4:30 pm
5:00 pm	5:30 pm
6:00 pm	6:30 pm
7:00 pm	7:30 pm
8:00 pm	8:30 pm
9:00 pm	9:30 pm

DAY / DATE ______________________________

MY GOALS TODAY

____

____

____

____

____

____

NOTES

TIME BLOCKS

3:00 am	3:30 am
4:00 am	4:30 am
5:00 am	5:30 am
6:00 am	6:30 am
7:00 am	7:30 am
8:00 am	8:30 am
9:00 am	9:30 am
10:00 am	10:30 am
11:00 am	11:30 am
12:00 pm	12:30 pm
1:00 pm	1:30 pm
2:00 pm	2:30 pm
3:00 pm	3:30 pm
4:00 pm	4:30 pm
5:00 pm	5:30 pm
6:00 pm	6:30 pm
7:00 pm	7:30 pm
8:00 pm	8:30 pm
9:00 pm	9:30 pm

DAY / DATE ______________________________

MY GOALS TODAY

____

____

____

____

____

____

NOTES

TIME BLOCKS

3:00 am	3:30 am
4:00 am	4:30 am
5:00 am	5:30 am
6:00 am	6:30 am
7:00 am	7:30 am
8:00 am	8:30 am
9:00 am	9:30 am
10:00 am	10:30 am
11:00 am	11:30 am
12:00 pm	12:30 pm
1:00 pm	1:30 pm
2:00 pm	2:30 pm
3:00 pm	3:30 pm
4:00 pm	4:30 pm
5:00 pm	5:30 pm
6:00 pm	6:30 pm
7:00 pm	7:30 pm
8:00 pm	8:30 pm
9:00 pm	9:30 pm

DAY / DATE ______________________________

MY GOALS TODAY

____

____

____

____

____

____

NOTES

TIME BLOCKS

3:00 am	3:30 am
4:00 am	4:30 am
5:00 am	5:30 am
6:00 am	6:30 am
7:00 am	7:30 am
8:00 am	8:30 am
9:00 am	9:30 am
10:00 am	10:30 am
11:00 am	11:30 am
12:00 pm	12:30 pm
1:00 pm	1:30 pm
2:00 pm	2:30 pm
3:00 pm	3:30 pm
4:00 pm	4:30 pm
5:00 pm	5:30 pm
6:00 pm	6:30 pm
7:00 pm	7:30 pm
8:00 pm	8:30 pm
9:00 pm	9:30 pm

DAY / DATE ______________________________

MY GOALS TODAY

____
____
____
____
____
____

NOTES

TIME BLOCKS

3:00 am	3:30 am
4:00 am	4:30 am
5:00 am	5:30 am
6:00 am	6:30 am
7:00 am	7:30 am
8:00 am	8:30 am
9:00 am	9:30 am
10:00 am	10:30 am
11:00 am	11:30 am
12:00 pm	12:30 pm
1:00 pm	1:30 pm
2:00 pm	2:30 pm
3:00 pm	3:30 pm
4:00 pm	4:30 pm
5:00 pm	5:30 pm
6:00 pm	6:30 pm
7:00 pm	7:30 pm
8:00 pm	8:30 pm
9:00 pm	9:30 pm

DAY / DATE ____________________

MY GOALS TODAY

____

____

____

____

____

____

NOTES

TIME BLOCKS

3:00 am	3:30 am
4:00 am	4:30 am
5:00 am	5:30 am
6:00 am	6:30 am
7:00 am	7:30 am
8:00 am	8:30 am
9:00 am	9:30 am
10:00 am	10:30 am
11:00 am	11:30 am
12:00 pm	12:30 pm
1:00 pm	1:30 pm
2:00 pm	2:30 pm
3:00 pm	3:30 pm
4:00 pm	4:30 pm
5:00 pm	5:30 pm
6:00 pm	6:30 pm
7:00 pm	7:30 pm
8:00 pm	8:30 pm
9:00 pm	9:30 pm

DAY / DATE ______________________________

MY GOALS TODAY

____

____

____

____

____

____

NOTES

TIME BLOCKS

3:00 am	3:30 am
4:00 am	4:30 am
5:00 am	5:30 am
6:00 am	6:30 am
7:00 am	7:30 am
8:00 am	8:30 am
9:00 am	9:30 am
10:00 am	10:30 am
11:00 am	11:30 am
12:00 pm	12:30 pm
1:00 pm	1:30 pm
2:00 pm	2:30 pm
3:00 pm	3:30 pm
4:00 pm	4:30 pm
5:00 pm	5:30 pm
6:00 pm	6:30 pm
7:00 pm	7:30 pm
8:00 pm	8:30 pm
9:00 pm	9:30 pm

DAY / DATE ______________________________

MY GOALS TODAY

____

____

____

____

____

____

NOTES

TIME BLOCKS

3:00 am	3:30 am
4:00 am	4:30 am
5:00 am	5:30 am
6:00 am	6:30 am
7:00 am	7:30 am
8:00 am	8:30 am
9:00 am	9:30 am
10:00 am	10:30 am
11:00 am	11:30 am
12:00 pm	12:30 pm
1:00 pm	1:30 pm
2:00 pm	2:30 pm
3:00 pm	3:30 pm
4:00 pm	4:30 pm
5:00 pm	5:30 pm
6:00 pm	6:30 pm
7:00 pm	7:30 pm
8:00 pm	8:30 pm
9:00 pm	9:30 pm

DAY / DATE ____________________

MY GOALS TODAY

NOTES

TIME BLOCKS

3:00 am	3:30 am
4:00 am	4:30 am
5:00 am	5:30 am
6:00 am	6:30 am
7:00 am	7:30 am
8:00 am	8:30 am
9:00 am	9:30 am
10:00 am	10:30 am
11:00 am	11:30 am
12:00 pm	12:30 pm
1:00 pm	1:30 pm
2:00 pm	2:30 pm
3:00 pm	3:30 pm
4:00 pm	4:30 pm
5:00 pm	5:30 pm
6:00 pm	6:30 pm
7:00 pm	7:30 pm
8:00 pm	8:30 pm
9:00 pm	9:30 pm

DAY / DATE ____________________

MY GOALS TODAY

____
____
____
____
____
____

NOTES

TIME BLOCKS

3:00 am	3:30 am
4:00 am	4:30 am
5:00 am	5:30 am
6:00 am	6:30 am
7:00 am	7:30 am
8:00 am	8:30 am
9:00 am	9:30 am
10:00 am	10:30 am
11:00 am	11:30 am
12:00 pm	12:30 pm
1:00 pm	1:30 pm
2:00 pm	2:30 pm
3:00 pm	3:30 pm
4:00 pm	4:30 pm
5:00 pm	5:30 pm
6:00 pm	6:30 pm
7:00 pm	7:30 pm
8:00 pm	8:30 pm
9:00 pm	9:30 pm

Thoughts become words. Words become action. Actions become character. Character becomes destiny.

DAY / DATE ______________________________

MY GOALS TODAY

____

____

____

____

____

____

NOTES

TIME BLOCKS

3:00 am	3:30 am
4:00 am	4:30 am
5:00 am	5:30 am
6:00 am	6:30 am
7:00 am	7:30 am
8:00 am	8:30 am
9:00 am	9:30 am
10:00 am	10:30 am
11:00 am	11:30 am
12:00 pm	12:30 pm
1:00 pm	1:30 pm
2:00 pm	2:30 pm
3:00 pm	3:30 pm
4:00 pm	4:30 pm
5:00 pm	5:30 pm
6:00 pm	6:30 pm
7:00 pm	7:30 pm
8:00 pm	8:30 pm
9:00 pm	9:30 pm

DAY / DATE ______________________________

MY GOALS TODAY

____

____

____

____

____

____

NOTES

TIME BLOCKS

3:00 am	3:30 am
4:00 am	4:30 am
5:00 am	5:30 am
6:00 am	6:30 am
7:00 am	7:30 am
8:00 am	8:30 am
9:00 am	9:30 am
10:00 am	10:30 am
11:00 am	11:30 am
12:00 pm	12:30 pm
1:00 pm	1:30 pm
2:00 pm	2:30 pm
3:00 pm	3:30 pm
4:00 pm	4:30 pm
5:00 pm	5:30 pm
6:00 pm	6:30 pm
7:00 pm	7:30 pm
8:00 pm	8:30 pm
9:00 pm	9:30 pm

DAY / DATE ______________________________

MY GOALS TODAY

____

____

____

____

____

____

NOTES

TIME BLOCKS

3:00 am	3:30 am
4:00 am	4:30 am
5:00 am	5:30 am
6:00 am	6:30 am
7:00 am	7:30 am
8:00 am	8:30 am
9:00 am	9:30 am
10:00 am	10:30 am
11:00 am	11:30 am
12:00 pm	12:30 pm
1:00 pm	1:30 pm
2:00 pm	2:30 pm
3:00 pm	3:30 pm
4:00 pm	4:30 pm
5:00 pm	5:30 pm
6:00 pm	6:30 pm
7:00 pm	7:30 pm
8:00 pm	8:30 pm
9:00 pm	9:30 pm

DAY / DATE ______________________________

MY GOALS TODAY

____

____

____

____

____

____

NOTES

TIME BLOCKS

3:00 am	3:30 am
4:00 am	4:30 am
5:00 am	5:30 am
6:00 am	6:30 am
7:00 am	7:30 am
8:00 am	8:30 am
9:00 am	9:30 am
10:00 am	10:30 am
11:00 am	11:30 am
12:00 pm	12:30 pm
1:00 pm	1:30 pm
2:00 pm	2:30 pm
3:00 pm	3:30 pm
4:00 pm	4:30 pm
5:00 pm	5:30 pm
6:00 pm	6:30 pm
7:00 pm	7:30 pm
8:00 pm	8:30 pm
9:00 pm	9:30 pm

DAY / DATE ______________________________

MY GOALS TODAY

____

____

____

____

____

____

NOTES

TIME BLOCKS

3:00 am	3:30 am
4:00 am	4:30 am
5:00 am	5:30 am
6:00 am	6:30 am
7:00 am	7:30 am
8:00 am	8:30 am
9:00 am	9:30 am
10:00 am	10:30 am
11:00 am	11:30 am
12:00 pm	12:30 pm
1:00 pm	1:30 pm
2:00 pm	2:30 pm
3:00 pm	3:30 pm
4:00 pm	4:30 pm
5:00 pm	5:30 pm
6:00 pm	6:30 pm
7:00 pm	7:30 pm
8:00 pm	8:30 pm
9:00 pm	9:30 pm

DAY / DATE ______________________________

MY GOALS TODAY

____
____
____
____
____
____

NOTES

TIME BLOCKS

3:00 am	3:30 am
4:00 am	4:30 am
5:00 am	5:30 am
6:00 am	6:30 am
7:00 am	7:30 am
8:00 am	8:30 am
9:00 am	9:30 am
10:00 am	10:30 am
11:00 am	11:30 am
12:00 pm	12:30 pm
1:00 pm	1:30 pm
2:00 pm	2:30 pm
3:00 pm	3:30 pm
4:00 pm	4:30 pm
5:00 pm	5:30 pm
6:00 pm	6:30 pm
7:00 pm	7:30 pm
8:00 pm	8:30 pm
9:00 pm	9:30 pm

DAY / DATE ______________________________

MY GOALS TODAY

____

____

____

____

____

____

NOTES

TIME BLOCKS

3:00 am	3:30 am
4:00 am	4:30 am
5:00 am	5:30 am
6:00 am	6:30 am
7:00 am	7:30 am
8:00 am	8:30 am
9:00 am	9:30 am
10:00 am	10:30 am
11:00 am	11:30 am
12:00 pm	12:30 pm
1:00 pm	1:30 pm
2:00 pm	2:30 pm
3:00 pm	3:30 pm
4:00 pm	4:30 pm
5:00 pm	5:30 pm
6:00 pm	6:30 pm
7:00 pm	7:30 pm
8:00 pm	8:30 pm
9:00 pm	9:30 pm

DAY / DATE ______________________________

MY GOALS TODAY

____
____
____
____
____
____

NOTES

TIME BLOCKS

3:00 am	3:30 am
4:00 am	4:30 am
5:00 am	5:30 am
6:00 am	6:30 am
7:00 am	7:30 am
8:00 am	8:30 am
9:00 am	9:30 am
10:00 am	10:30 am
11:00 am	11:30 am
12:00 pm	12:30 pm
1:00 pm	1:30 pm
2:00 pm	2:30 pm
3:00 pm	3:30 pm
4:00 pm	4:30 pm
5:00 pm	5:30 pm
6:00 pm	6:30 pm
7:00 pm	7:30 pm
8:00 pm	8:30 pm
9:00 pm	9:30 pm

DAY / DATE ______________________________

MY GOALS TODAY

____

____

____

____

____

____

NOTES

TIME BLOCKS

3:00 am	3:30 am
4:00 am	4:30 am
5:00 am	5:30 am
6:00 am	6:30 am
7:00 am	7:30 am
8:00 am	8:30 am
9:00 am	9:30 am
10:00 am	10:30 am
11:00 am	11:30 am
12:00 pm	12:30 pm
1:00 pm	1:30 pm
2:00 pm	2:30 pm
3:00 pm	3:30 pm
4:00 pm	4:30 pm
5:00 pm	5:30 pm
6:00 pm	6:30 pm
7:00 pm	7:30 pm
8:00 pm	8:30 pm
9:00 pm	9:30 pm

DAY / DATE ______________________

MY GOALS TODAY

____

____

____

____

____

____

NOTES

TIME BLOCKS

3:00 am	3:30 am
4:00 am	4:30 am
5:00 am	5:30 am
6:00 am	6:30 am
7:00 am	7:30 am
8:00 am	8:30 am
9:00 am	9:30 am
10:00 am	10:30 am
11:00 am	11:30 am
12:00 pm	12:30 pm
1:00 pm	1:30 pm
2:00 pm	2:30 pm
3:00 pm	3:30 pm
4:00 pm	4:30 pm
5:00 pm	5:30 pm
6:00 pm	6:30 pm
7:00 pm	7:30 pm
8:00 pm	8:30 pm
9:00 pm	9:30 pm

DAY / DATE ______________________________

MY GOALS TODAY

____

____

____

____

____

____

NOTES

TIME BLOCKS

3:00 am	3:30 am
4:00 am	4:30 am
5:00 am	5:30 am
6:00 am	6:30 am
7:00 am	7:30 am
8:00 am	8:30 am
9:00 am	9:30 am
10:00 am	10:30 am
11:00 am	11:30 am
12:00 pm	12:30 pm
1:00 pm	1:30 pm
2:00 pm	2:30 pm
3:00 pm	3:30 pm
4:00 pm	4:30 pm
5:00 pm	5:30 pm
6:00 pm	6:30 pm
7:00 pm	7:30 pm
8:00 pm	8:30 pm
9:00 pm	9:30 pm

DAY / DATE ____________________

MY GOALS TODAY

TIME BLOCKS

3:00 am	3:30 am
4:00 am	4:30 am
5:00 am	5:30 am
6:00 am	6:30 am
7:00 am	7:30 am
8:00 am	8:30 am
9:00 am	9:30 am
10:00 am	10:30 am
11:00 am	11:30 am
12:00 pm	12:30 pm
1:00 pm	1:30 pm
2:00 pm	2:30 pm
3:00 pm	3:30 pm
4:00 pm	4:30 pm
5:00 pm	5:30 pm
6:00 pm	6:30 pm
7:00 pm	7:30 pm
8:00 pm	8:30 pm
9:00 pm	9:30 pm

NOTES

DAY / DATE ______________________________

MY GOALS TODAY

____
____
____
____
____
____

NOTES

TIME BLOCKS

3:00 am	3:30 am
4:00 am	4:30 am
5:00 am	5:30 am
6:00 am	6:30 am
7:00 am	7:30 am
8:00 am	8:30 am
9:00 am	9:30 am
10:00 am	10:30 am
11:00 am	11:30 am
12:00 pm	12:30 pm
1:00 pm	1:30 pm
2:00 pm	2:30 pm
3:00 pm	3:30 pm
4:00 pm	4:30 pm
5:00 pm	5:30 pm
6:00 pm	6:30 pm
7:00 pm	7:30 pm
8:00 pm	8:30 pm
9:00 pm	9:30 pm

DAY / DATE ______________________________

MY GOALS TODAY

____
____
____
____
____
____

NOTES

TIME BLOCKS

3:00 am	3:30 am
4:00 am	4:30 am
5:00 am	5:30 am
6:00 am	6:30 am
7:00 am	7:30 am
8:00 am	8:30 am
9:00 am	9:30 am
10:00 am	10:30 am
11:00 am	11:30 am
12:00 pm	12:30 pm
1:00 pm	1:30 pm
2:00 pm	2:30 pm
3:00 pm	3:30 pm
4:00 pm	4:30 pm
5:00 pm	5:30 pm
6:00 pm	6:30 pm
7:00 pm	7:30 pm
8:00 pm	8:30 pm
9:00 pm	9:30 pm

DAY / DATE ____________________

MY GOALS TODAY

____

____

____

____

____

____

NOTES

TIME BLOCKS

3:00 am	3:30 am
4:00 am	4:30 am
5:00 am	5:30 am
6:00 am	6:30 am
7:00 am	7:30 am
8:00 am	8:30 am
9:00 am	9:30 am
10:00 am	10:30 am
11:00 am	11:30 am
12:00 pm	12:30 pm
1:00 pm	1:30 pm
2:00 pm	2:30 pm
3:00 pm	3:30 pm
4:00 pm	4:30 pm
5:00 pm	5:30 pm
6:00 pm	6:30 pm
7:00 pm	7:30 pm
8:00 pm	8:30 pm
9:00 pm	9:30 pm

DAY / DATE ______________________________

MY GOALS TODAY

____

____

____

____

____

____

NOTES

TIME BLOCKS

3:00 am	3:30 am
4:00 am	4:30 am
5:00 am	5:30 am
6:00 am	6:30 am
7:00 am	7:30 am
8:00 am	8:30 am
9:00 am	9:30 am
10:00 am	10:30 am
11:00 am	11:30 am
12:00 pm	12:30 pm
1:00 pm	1:30 pm
2:00 pm	2:30 pm
3:00 pm	3:30 pm
4:00 pm	4:30 pm
5:00 pm	5:30 pm
6:00 pm	6:30 pm
7:00 pm	7:30 pm
8:00 pm	8:30 pm
9:00 pm	9:30 pm

DAY / DATE ______________________________

MY GOALS TODAY

____

____

____

____

____

____

NOTES

TIME BLOCKS

3:00 am	3:30 am
4:00 am	4:30 am
5:00 am	5:30 am
6:00 am	6:30 am
7:00 am	7:30 am
8:00 am	8:30 am
9:00 am	9:30 am
10:00 am	10:30 am
11:00 am	11:30 am
12:00 pm	12:30 pm
1:00 pm	1:30 pm
2:00 pm	2:30 pm
3:00 pm	3:30 pm
4:00 pm	4:30 pm
5:00 pm	5:30 pm
6:00 pm	6:30 pm
7:00 pm	7:30 pm
8:00 pm	8:30 pm
9:00 pm	9:30 pm

DAY / DATE ______________________________

MY GOALS TODAY

____
____
____
____
____
____

NOTES

TIME BLOCKS

3:00 am	3:30 am
4:00 am	4:30 am
5:00 am	5:30 am
6:00 am	6:30 am
7:00 am	7:30 am
8:00 am	8:30 am
9:00 am	9:30 am
10:00 am	10:30 am
11:00 am	11:30 am
12:00 pm	12:30 pm
1:00 pm	1:30 pm
2:00 pm	2:30 pm
3:00 pm	3:30 pm
4:00 pm	4:30 pm
5:00 pm	5:30 pm
6:00 pm	6:30 pm
7:00 pm	7:30 pm
8:00 pm	8:30 pm
9:00 pm	9:30 pm

DAY / DATE ______________________________

MY GOALS TODAY

____

____

____

____

____

____

NOTES

TIME BLOCKS

3:00 am	3:30 am
4:00 am	4:30 am
5:00 am	5:30 am
6:00 am	6:30 am
7:00 am	7:30 am
8:00 am	8:30 am
9:00 am	9:30 am
10:00 am	10:30 am
11:00 am	11:30 am
12:00 pm	12:30 pm
1:00 pm	1:30 pm
2:00 pm	2:30 pm
3:00 pm	3:30 pm
4:00 pm	4:30 pm
5:00 pm	5:30 pm
6:00 pm	6:30 pm
7:00 pm	7:30 pm
8:00 pm	8:30 pm
9:00 pm	9:30 pm

DAY / DATE ______________________

MY GOALS TODAY

____

____

____

____

____

____

NOTES

TIME BLOCKS

3:00 am	3:30 am
4:00 am	4:30 am
5:00 am	5:30 am
6:00 am	6:30 am
7:00 am	7:30 am
8:00 am	8:30 am
9:00 am	9:30 am
10:00 am	10:30 am
11:00 am	11:30 am
12:00 pm	12:30 pm
1:00 pm	1:30 pm
2:00 pm	2:30 pm
3:00 pm	3:30 pm
4:00 pm	4:30 pm
5:00 pm	5:30 pm
6:00 pm	6:30 pm
7:00 pm	7:30 pm
8:00 pm	8:30 pm
9:00 pm	9:30 pm

DAY / DATE ____________________

MY GOALS TODAY

____

____

____

____

____

____

NOTES

TIME BLOCKS

3:00 am	3:30 am
4:00 am	4:30 am
5:00 am	5:30 am
6:00 am	6:30 am
7:00 am	7:30 am
8:00 am	8:30 am
9:00 am	9:30 am
10:00 am	10:30 am
11:00 am	11:30 am
12:00 pm	12:30 pm
1:00 pm	1:30 pm
2:00 pm	2:30 pm
3:00 pm	3:30 pm
4:00 pm	4:30 pm
5:00 pm	5:30 pm
6:00 pm	6:30 pm
7:00 pm	7:30 pm
8:00 pm	8:30 pm
9:00 pm	9:30 pm

DAY / DATE ____________________

MY GOALS TODAY

____
____
____
____
____
____

NOTES

TIME BLOCKS

3:00 am	3:30 am
4:00 am	4:30 am
5:00 am	5:30 am
6:00 am	6:30 am
7:00 am	7:30 am
8:00 am	8:30 am
9:00 am	9:30 am
10:00 am	10:30 am
11:00 am	11:30 am
12:00 pm	12:30 pm
1:00 pm	1:30 pm
2:00 pm	2:30 pm
3:00 pm	3:30 pm
4:00 pm	4:30 pm
5:00 pm	5:30 pm
6:00 pm	6:30 pm
7:00 pm	7:30 pm
8:00 pm	8:30 pm
9:00 pm	9:30 pm

DAY / DATE ______________________________

MY GOALS TODAY

____
____
____
____
____
____

NOTES

TIME BLOCKS

3:00 am	3:30 am
4:00 am	4:30 am
5:00 am	5:30 am
6:00 am	6:30 am
7:00 am	7:30 am
8:00 am	8:30 am
9:00 am	9:30 am
10:00 am	10:30 am
11:00 am	11:30 am
12:00 pm	12:30 pm
1:00 pm	1:30 pm
2:00 pm	2:30 pm
3:00 pm	3:30 pm
4:00 pm	4:30 pm
5:00 pm	5:30 pm
6:00 pm	6:30 pm
7:00 pm	7:30 pm
8:00 pm	8:30 pm
9:00 pm	9:30 pm

DAY / DATE ____________________

MY GOALS TODAY

____

____

____

____

____

____

NOTES

TIME BLOCKS

3:00 am	3:30 am
4:00 am	4:30 am
5:00 am	5:30 am
6:00 am	6:30 am
7:00 am	7:30 am
8:00 am	8:30 am
9:00 am	9:30 am
10:00 am	10:30 am
11:00 am	11:30 am
12:00 pm	12:30 pm
1:00 pm	1:30 pm
2:00 pm	2:30 pm
3:00 pm	3:30 pm
4:00 pm	4:30 pm
5:00 pm	5:30 pm
6:00 pm	6:30 pm
7:00 pm	7:30 pm
8:00 pm	8:30 pm
9:00 pm	9:30 pm

DAY / DATE ______________________________

MY GOALS TODAY

____
____
____
____
____
____

NOTES

TIME BLOCKS

3:00 am	3:30 am
4:00 am	4:30 am
5:00 am	5:30 am
6:00 am	6:30 am
7:00 am	7:30 am
8:00 am	8:30 am
9:00 am	9:30 am
10:00 am	10:30 am
11:00 am	11:30 am
12:00 pm	12:30 pm
1:00 pm	1:30 pm
2:00 pm	2:30 pm
3:00 pm	3:30 pm
4:00 pm	4:30 pm
5:00 pm	5:30 pm
6:00 pm	6:30 pm
7:00 pm	7:30 pm
8:00 pm	8:30 pm
9:00 pm	9:30 pm

Made in the USA
Monee, IL
08 November 2026

68028674R00208